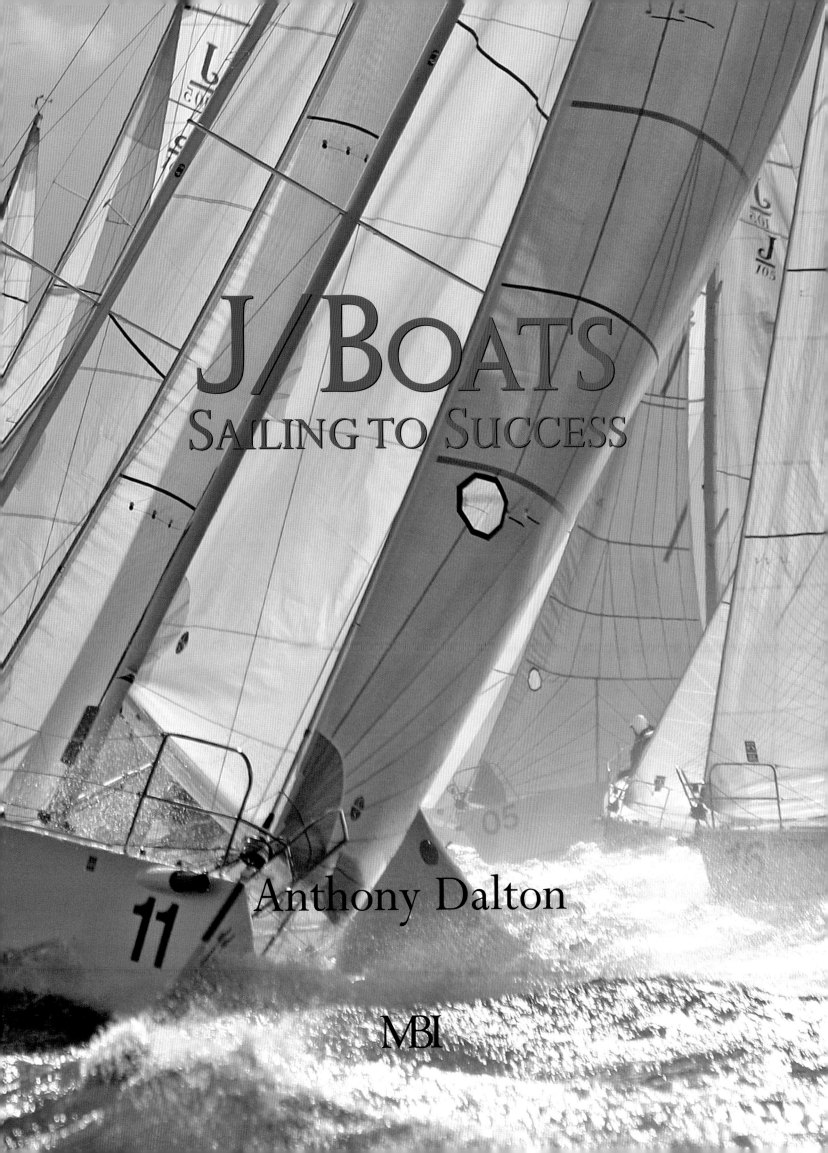

J/Boats
Sailing to Success

Anthony Dalton

MBI

First published in 2005 by MBI, an imprint of MBI Publishing Company, Galtier Plaza, Suite 200, 380 Jackson Street, St. Paul, MN 55101-3885 USA

The information in this book is true and complete to the best of our knowledge. All recommendations are made without any guarantee on the part of the author or Publisher, who also disclaim any liability incurred in connection with the use of this data or specific details.

This publication has not been prepared, approved, or licensed by J/Boats, Inc. We recognize, further, that some words, model names, and designations mentioned herein are the property of the trademark holder. We use them for identification purposes only. This is not an official publication.

MBI titles are also available at discounts in bulk quantity for industrial or sales-promotional use. For details write to Special Sales Manager at MBI Publishing Company, Galtier Plaza, Suite 200, 380 Jackson Street, St. Paul, MN 55101-3885 USA.

ISBN-13: 978-0-7603-2170-6
ISBN-10: 0-7603-2170-1

Library of Congress Cataloging-in-Publication Data

Dalton, Anthony.
    J/Boats: sailing to success/by Anthony Dalton
        p. cm.
    ISBN: 0-7603-2170-1
        1.J/Boats, Inc. 2. Yacht building—United States—History—20th century. 3. Boatbuilding—United States—History—20th centruy. 4. Sailboats—United States. 5. Yachts—United States. I. Title.

    VM321.52.U6D35 2005
    623.822'3—dc22

Printed in China

On the front cover: Steve Hollis' J/105 *Sirocco* in blustery conditions during the Sunday race of the 2004 J/105 North American Championship at Marion, Massachusetts. *Hoss*, based in Dallas/Ft. Worth, Texas, was the overall winner of the six-race event.

Endpaper: A cruising version of the J/34, the J/34c makes for an ideal long-distance voyaging and live-aboard boat. One couple sailed the Caribbean for two years in comfort on their J/34c.

On the frontispiece: Anchoring within swimming distance of pristine beaches and shady palms draws cruisers to the Caribbean and the South Pacific.

On the title page: A tightly packed fleet of J/105s rounds a mark during the J/105 North American Championship at Marion, Massachusetts, in 2004.

On the contents page: A fleet of J/105s, the first J/Sprit boats, races at San Francisco in 2000.

On the back cover: Rod Johnstone's intent was to design a boat that could beat other boats upwind as well as downwind. He achieved his goal with his first production boat, the J/24. It was awarded International Class status in 1981.

Editors: Lindsay Hitch and Dennis Pernu
Designer: Christopher Fayers

Contents

Acknowledgments

One of the joys of researching a nonfiction book is the people you meet on the long journey from concept to completed volume. When Dennis Pernu, my editor at MBI Publishing Company, phoned and asked me if I would take on this project, I had mixed emotions. On the one hand, I was delighted at the implied compliment. On the other, I couldn't help but be concerned at the daunting task before me because, although I am a reasonably experienced sailor, I have never raced and, to me at the time, J/Boats equated to racing boats. My fears proved groundless. Over a period of six months, I came to know many members of the extended Johnstone family by telephone, e-mails, and in some cases in person. That extended Johnstone family is a large one. Often I felt I should have a Johnstone family tree in front of me as a guide to the next person on my list and their relationship to Rod Johnstone.

My sincere thanks are due to all at J/Boats, Inc. for putting up with my probing questions. Jeff and Alan Johnstone allowed me to tape our conversations, and Jeff opened up the company's vast picture files for me. Rod Johnstone graciously took me on a tour of Pearson Composites in Warren, Rhode Island, where a high proportion of Js are built, and he patiently explained the complicated construction processes in terms I could understand. Rod also loaned me his photo collection from the days when he built the first J boat in his garage. On a subsequent visit to Newport, Bob Johnstone kindly invited me to be his guest at the New York Yacht Club's Harbour Court. There, overlooking a wintry sea, we taped many hours of conversation about J/Boats. Jeff, Rod, and Bob Johnstone also read much of the manuscript, corrected my errors, and suggested useful changes and additions. Any remaining errors are mine. Lucia, John, Phil, Stuart, and Drake Johnstone gave up their valuable time to answer my questions, as did Everett Pearson and Ken Read. Phil Johnstone also checked parts of the manuscript. Sailmaker Sandy Van Zandt responded quickly to my e-mailed request for information.

I am indebted to many owners of varying sizes of J boats for sharing their thoughts and experiences with me. In particular, I must single out Tom and Jane Babbitt; Ben Blake and two of his three sons, Adam and Morgan; Steve Blecher; Dr. Scott Piper; Ned Cabot; John Eills; and Richard York; plus Eric Cressy – publisher of *SAIL* magazine. Thanks also to J/Boats employees Kendra Muenter and Marilyn Murphy for their assistance with information, and for acting as my chauffer on one occasion.

My thanks to associate editor Lindsay Hitch for her thoughtful advice and editing skills. Once again, I have enjoyed working with Dennis Pernu. I would like to extend my heartfelt thanks to him for offering me the opportunity of preparing this book.

Bob Johnstone's personal J/24, *Top of the World*, sits at anchor in a cove off Narragansett Bay, Newport, Rhode Island. Bob and his crew raced the bright red J/24 in many events, both national and local.

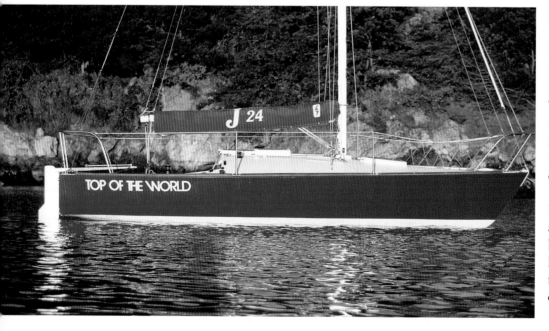

Introduction

The New England states have generated some of the finest boat designers and builders the world has ever seen. The Herreshoff family of Rhode Island produced at least six, starting with Nathanael Greene Herreshoff and his blind brother, John Brown Herreshoff. The Herreshoffs were America's boat-building royalty when wooden boats ruled the waves up to the mid-1900s.

With the advent of fiberglass, a construction medium Nat Herreshoff's son L. Francis Herreshoff unkindly referred to as "frozen snot," a new breed of boat designers and builders came to the fore. Among them, none stands out as boldly as Everett Pearson, a Rhode Islander transplanted from New York. Although he was not the first builder of fiberglass boats, he certainly could claim the distinction of having built the first production boats.

Now recognized as the grandfather of fiberglass boat building, Pearson has built over 10,000 fiberglass boats in a career spanning more than 45 years. It's not surprising, therefore, that the name of Everett Pearson became linked with that of Rod Johnstone in the early days of the latter's first serious boat-building effort. Johnstone, designer of the supremely successful J/24, as well as a long line of other racers and cruisers, is not a native New Englander either. He was born in New Jersey, but has lived in Connecticut for more than 40 years; most of that time in Stonington, right beside the border with Rhode Island. The Johnstone family had been spending summers in the Stonington area for decades.

Rod Johnstone's grandfather, Robert L. Johnstone, bought two islands off Stonington in the 1920s. He would take his family there

The J/24 was the first production boat Rod Johnstone designed. Today, there are in excess of 5,400 of these 24-foot racing sloops in dozens of club fleets throughout the world.

each summer, until he decided that owning two islands with a house on each was a waste. Unable to decide which one to keep and which one to sell, he put them both on the market, planning to keep whichever one did not sell first. "Salt Acres," the surviving property, subsequently remained in the family until 1995. Rod's parents, Robert Legrand Johnstone Jr. and Elizabeth Van Liew Johnstone, took their four children to Salt Acres most summers.

The western reaches of the Atlantic Ocean, an irresistible draw for local sailors, had a similar impact on the Johnstones. Perhaps the fresh New England air—aided and abetted by salty Atlantic winds, alternately playful and stormy—is responsible for releasing the outstanding boat design and building talents of its residents. The Herreshoffs introduced their classic boats to New England waters in 1878. A little less than 100 years later, the Johnstone name began to make itself known as a boating force to be reckoned with when Rod Johnstone hoisted sails on his home-built 24-foot boat to win a summer of races. And that was just the beginning.

The current J/Boats, Inc. offices on Thames Street in Newport, Rhode Island.

J/Boats, Inc., the company Rod and his older brother, Bob, founded, is based close to the waterfront in the old town of Newport, Rhode Island, only a few miles from Stonington, and many of the boats are built a little farther inland in Warren, Rhode Island.

The enormous worldwide popularity of the designs in the now-extensive J/Boats line is the result of what has been called "a classic entrepreneurial tale." One brother built a small sailboat in his garage. It proved to be something of a greyhound. His older brother joined him, with a financial investment, and J/Boats was born.

Less than three decades later, that fast and sea-kindly prototype sailboat, the J/24, has—according to the company's abundant archival information— become the most popular recreational keelboat in the world. The success of the J/24 spawned a long list of 36 designs, ranging from 22 to 65 feet. Among them is a stunning mix of winning racers and family-friendly cruisers. Family owned and family run, in less than 30 years the company has grown to the extent that it is now the unquestioned leader of high-quality, one-design sailboats in America, if not the world.

Producing a book on the history of such a young company may seem somewhat premature, but this is no ordinary company, and the Johnstones are no ordinary family. This book is the story of the realization of one man's dream to become a yacht designer. It is the story of how a family united to combine its nautical and business talents to build a yachting dynasty. It is the story of J/Boats, Inc.

Robert and Libby Johnstone, parents of Bob and Rod Johnstone, at Salt Acres, the family's summer home on an island off Stonington, Connecticut.

The list of boat designs put in production by J/Boats in less than three decades numbers 36. The magnificent J/160 cruiser/racer seen here with spinnaker set joined the fleet in 1995.

J/160s have roamed all over the world since the design was unveiled in 1995. A nearly identical boat to this one has circumnavigated three times and is now on a fourth 'round-the-world voyage.

J/105s in action on San Francisco Bay. J/Boats introduced the carbon-fiber retractable bowsprit with the J/105. It is clearly visible on the lead boat.

One

Introducing *Ragtime*

" **I** just wanted a sailboat for myself and my family, but along the way it turned into a great adventure—a collective effort involving not only me, my family, and friends, but thousands of sailors all over the world," wrote Rod Johnstone, designer of the enormously successful J/24 racing keelboat.

Johnstone's father, Robert, was Rod's inspiration. Robert, a sailor and a racer who could not afford to buy a boat of his own, took the initiative, and using purchased plans, built one in his garage with help from two of his sons, 9-year-old Rodney and 12-year-old Bob. That 19-foot Lightning Class sloop—number 3310, named *Prodigal III*—became the vehicle in which Rod and his older brother, Bob, plus younger brother, John, learned to sail and to win races. It also sparked an interest in Rod's mind.

Opposite page:
Father and teenage son, Rod and Jeff Johnstone, teamed up to race their Olympic 470 dinghy in the summers of 1973 and 1974, after Rod's wife, Lucia, gave up the sport.

Rod Johnstone built the 24-foot *Ragtime* in one snug bay of his three-car garage in Stonington, Connecticut. When he pulled out the completed hull, it scratched the door jambs on either side.

At 12 years old Rod designed and built a model sloop 2 feet long, the first of many. Throughout his teenage school years and during summer jobs as a sailing instructor while home from Princeton University, he continued to exercise his skills by repairing and maintaining boats. Once out of Princeton with a degree in history and his military service behind him, Rod married Frannie Davis and became a family man. While teaching history in Millbrook, New York, and raising two sons, Jeff and Phil, he exercised his passion for boats and boat design by enrolling in a correspondence course at Westlawn School of Yacht Design. That course taught him the basics of designing small craft under 100 feet in length. It would prove to be a fortuitous educational experience. In July 1962, the family moved to Stonington, Connecticut, close to where his parents had taken him and his brothers and sister during summer vacations. In Stonington, Rod and Frannie planned to bring up their children while Rod pursued a career as a yacht designer.

Rod admitted, "It took me fifteen years to get my act together and realize that I am really good at what I always wanted to do, and that is designing sailboats."

Having the desire to design yachts, even when combined with a successful course in boat design, did not guarantee a solid future in the sailboat world. For the rest of the 1960s, Rod had to work full-time at a day job and relegate sailboat design to hobby status. For three years, he ran a yacht brokerage at Dodson Boat Yard in Stonington. In 1965, he went to work at the Electric Boat Division of General Dynamics in Groton, Connecticut, where he planned and scheduled the installation of components and equipment on nuclear

Rod Johnstone fairs *Ragtime*'s keel. For many months, it stood in a cradle outside Rod's garage waiting to be attached to the hull.

submarines. When he had time, he also designed sailboats for himself, but still only as a nonpaying hobby. Rod and Frannie had three more children during this period—Alan, Becky, and Pam. The demands of work and a large family obviously left little time for a hobby, and there were other problems. The marriage suffered too much from the tension and stress of that period and failed. The couple divorced in 1969.

Although Rod had pushed his dream of designing sailboats into a holding pattern for some time, it never left his mind. In 1970, he resigned from General Dynamics and, with financial backing, started a sailing school in Essex, Connecticut. Johnstone's backers in that endeavor owned *Soundings*, a monthly boating newspaper. At the end of the first summer sailing season when the school closed for the winter, *Soundings* gave Rod a job selling display advertising. That was possibly the single most useful experience in his diverse working career. As a result of selling advertising over the next six years, he met many important figures from the boating industry. Among them, and most important for Johnstone, was Everett Pearson, president of Tillotson-Pearson, Inc., from Warren, Rhode Island.

Pearson, known affectionately as "the grandfather of fiberglass boat building," had

garnered a nationwide reputation for excellence in fiberglass boat construction, having built his first such boat in 1955.

In 1971, Rod married Lucia Trowbridge, adding her two young children, Robert and Ashley, to his own five. A year later, he moved the expanded family to a larger house in Stonington, which conveniently had a three car garage. In 1973, he designed and built a 9-foot fiberglass rowing/sailing dinghy with some help from his second son, Phil, and a lot more from his 11-year-old son, Alan, who named the boat *Wizard*. Rod's oldest brother, Bob, contributed by sending them an old Penguin sail, which Rod and Alan cut down to fit the dinghy's rig. Alan learned to race on *Wizard* and he learned to win while competing in the Stonington Harbor Wednesday night races.

Family, friends, and neighbors collected at the Johnstones' garage in May 1976 to lend their muscles at a "hull-raising party" to lift *Ragtime* and place her on her keel.

The 25-strong group of family and friends who attended Rod's "hull-raising party" were surprised to discover how light and easy to manage *Ragtime*'s hull was.

With her keel finally attached, *Ragtime* is suspended in slings from the boat hoist prior to her launching on Saturday, May 15, 1976.

Rod's sailboat racing career had been on hold since the early 1960s. When he married Lucia, he took her sailing on a 505 sloop during their honeymoon in Bermuda. In the summer of 1972, he persuaded her to crew with him on their own 505 at several big regattas. Lucia got the all-important job of hanging out over the water on the trapeze. Unfortunately, she was too light "on the wire" for top-level competition, so they sold the boat and teamed up on a new Olympic 470 in 1973.

After a season of successful competition with the 470, Rod and Lucia sailed at the Canadian Olympic Regatta at Kingston, Ontario (CORK), on Lake Ontario. That week proved to be the hottest on record in local history, and there was very little wind. Lucia did not enjoy the week at all. It did not help that, as a crew, the two were too heavy to be competitive at the top level in a 470— Rod is 6 feet 1 inch and Lucia is 5 feet 8 inches. At the end of the week, after eight

hours a day wearing a wetsuit in humid conditions, Lucia swore she would never sail on a 470 again. Rod, of course, still wanted to race, so he turned to his oldest son, Jeff, who, at the tender age of 13, was already an accomplished racing skipper. And, to the new crew's advantage, Jeff only weighed 90 pounds.

Rod and Jeff raced together on the 470 from late 1973 to the summer of 1974. They had dreams of Olympic glory, but those dreams were short-lived, although they won many races in top competition. Rod explained, "It was one thing for Lucia and me to go away to a regatta, as a vacation away from the kids. That was an easy sell. But when I would take off sailing with Jeff and leave Lucia with the rest of the kids, our winning exploits got short shrift when we walked in the door after a regatta. Lucia was no longer part of it and wanted no part of it. So, it appeared that my competitive sailing days were over."

Rod was losing his would-be Olympic crew anyway. Jeff went away to school in

1974, and Rod sold the 470. It wasn't all bad. Rod then had the motivation he needed to start a new boat-building project, one that would get him back on the water and get the whole family sailing together. He had an ideal sailboat in mind, one he had actually started designing in 1964. That year, he had designed and built a 1:12 scale sailing model of a 24-foot offshore racing keelboat for Jeff, then five years old.

"It was my answer to the Cal 24, the hottest little cruiser/racer sloop of its day," Rod said. "I spent a lot of time chasing this little model around Stonington Harbor in a rowboat in the summer of 1965." That model became the basis for the hull of a boat Rod would eventually build a decade later.

In 1974, Rod sat down to design his ideal sailboat in earnest. Not having sufficient money to have the boat custom-built, he chose to build it himself at home and make it as large as he could fit into a 28-foot-deep garage with doors 9 feet wide. Given the space limitations, Rod made the overall dimensions of the boat design 24 feet LOA with a beam of 8 feet 11 inches.

In Rod's own words: "The design objective was clear: to create the largest, fastest boat we could build in the confines of our garage. I thought of the 505, which can plane upwind and down. My greatest challenge was to create a 24-footer with superior upwind speed, which means the boat needed its own inherent stability, as well as a wide hiking platform for the crew. I designed a 1,020-pound ballast keel to go with a hull that is narrow at the water line and beamy on deck because, unlike the 'Five-Oh,' there would be no trapezes and capsizing was not an option. We would have to compete against larger boats whose greater length made them theoretically faster upwind, especially in the strong currents of Fishers Island Sound. I was confident that the light displacement (2,400 pounds) and low wetted surface would make the boat fast downwind, even with a conservative, fractional-rig sail plan. Simplicity and easy sail handling for Lucia and the kids were important, so large headsails were out of the question. (Racing sail inventories for the masthead-rigged racing boats, which were popular at the time, were nearly double the size and cost of what we [eventually] had on *Ragtime*.) The boat had to be simple to build, because I had to build it. It had to be simple and safe to operate, because my crew was kind of green at the time. I have

Lucia Johnstone cracks a bottle of champagne over *Ragtime*'s bow on launching day. She recalled, "I forgot to wrap something around the bottle, so the glass and champagne went everywhere."

As *Ragtime* begins her descent into the water for the first time, the dedication and hours of work her designer and builders put into her are shown to advantage.

never liked running backstays on an offshore boat, and I have never thought that a masthead rig was sensible on anything less than 30 feet LOA."

Referring to the fiberglass *Wizard* Rod had designed and built in his basement, Phil said: "Dad was always designing, and tinkering with designs. So I'd go to the basement or wherever he was working and hang out with him, and he'd try and teach me something of what he was doing. I helped build the 9-footer in the early stages, and that boat was fast."

Rod Johnstone supervises *Ragtime*'s launch as she is carefully lowered into the harbor at Stonington, Connecticut.

As the slings are released, *Ragtime* is afloat and ready to have her mast stepped and rigged for a season of racing.

Discussing the idea of a new and bigger boat with his son a couple of years later, Rod asked, "So, Phil, what do you think?" Phil's answer was an unequivocal, "Go for it, Dad."

Even with Phil's youthful approval, Rod was concerned that such a big project might be too much of a disruption to the family life and too much of a drain on his financial resources. Phil's enthusiasm to go ahead with the work reflected that of everyone else in the family. Lucia certainly approved. She said, "It was a great project. We were all excited about having a competitive boat that would be fun for all of us."

Between October and December 1974, Rod lofted the lines. Construction started immediately after Christmas, on December 26, and progressed relatively smoothly. Just over two months later, the outer shell was laid up with the help of family and friends. Alan Johnstone, Rod's third son, who is now vice president and designer of J/Boats, Inc., recalled: "He [Rod] had a pretty big labor pool to draw from in those days. Building *Ragtime* was a real family effort. Everyone was involved at some time or other. My brother Phil really spent a lot more time helping my father than I ever did. But, when I wasn't out skateboarding with my buddies, I helped build the boat with my brothers and sisters."

After completing the outer fiberglass shell on the foam-cored hull and fairing the glass to a reasonable smoothness, someone had to remove the numerous screws holding the foam core to the temporary wooden pattern. Thirty years later, Becky, Pam, Ashley, Phil, Alan, and Rob all remember their father sending them under the boat, each equipped with a flashlight and screwdriver, to remove the screws. Pam remembers playing under the boat and being scolded once for doing so in her best Sunday dress. Lucia, who often helped work the fiberglass, related an argument she and Rod had about who was responsible for their prickly bed sheets a day after they had spent hours fiberglassing the hull. Likewise, Becky recalled having to take many showers to get fine fiberglass shards out of her hair.

For Phil the boat became an after-school project for a whole year. "I'd come home from school, particularly in winter when I had time on my hands, and go straight to work in the garage. Building *Ragtime* certainly took some time out of my youth. But it was a good way for me to work with my dad and hang out together."

Phil's jobs included assembling ribbing, and gluing and screwing foam core to it to make a mold. He also assisted in laying up the fiberglass. The family workforce received a boost as Rod's youngest brother, John, regularly drove up from Madison, Connecticut, to Stonington to help Rod build *Ragtime*. "I'd do odd jobs such as grinding or removing screws. Whatever was needed at the time," he said. John conceded that Rod did most of the work himself, although he was helped by many others, particularly Phil, who John jokingly referred to as "the fiberglass rat."

When it came to the difficult task of fairing the hull, Phil said his father found himself out of his depth. Rod circumvented that problem by hiring an expert to help and to teach him the correct way to finish a boat's hull.

With little money to spare, Rod had to build the boat on a shoestring budget. Lucia spoke of the generosity of family and friends in supplying materials as well as labor. Rod's oldest brother, Bob, came through with a care package, consisting of mostly old Harken blocks left over from his 1972 Soling Olympic campaign when he finished a respectable sixth. Rod had crewed for Bob on the same boat with Bob's wife, Mary, at the 1971 Soling World Championship. He said, "Some of the hardware that turned up in Stonington four years later looked vaguely familiar. It was all put to good use on *Ragtime*." In fact, much of that "care package" came from Bob's Soling, once owned by racing legend Paul Elvstrom.

Ben Hall, president of Hall Spars, recalled Rod talking to him about a mast when he [Ben] was working at Kenyon Spars. "We built the masts for the Etchells 22," Hall explained. "Rod thought the mast, with a slight modification, would be perfect for *Ragtime*. So we cut forty inches off the top of an Etchells 22 mast and that [the lower majority] became the first J/24's mast."

While he was building *Ragtime*, Rod enlisted the expertise of sailmaker Sandy Van Zandt. The two had been friendly competitors, sailing various classes of racing boats as far back as the mid-1960s.

"I started a sailmaking business, Van Zandt Sails, in Noank and later Old Mystic, specializing in racing sails back in the late '50s," said Van Zandt. "So Rodney, who was embarking on a career as a yacht designer, and I often talked about sails and rigs. Since the sails are the engine that powers a sailboat and will ultimately determine whether a design will perform up to her potential, it is a subject that commands a lot of attention."

Rod and Sandy discussed *Ragtime*'s design and the sail plan. "I felt that he needed to put some more sail area in the mainsail, and particularly on the foot to make certain that there would be sufficient weather helm to make the boat perform well in light air. We made these changes to the sail plan and the J/24 certainly sailed pretty much up to her potential 'right out of the starting blocks.'"

Rod Johnstone, *Ragtime*'s designer and builder, shows his pleasure after the successful launch of his new boat.

After many years racing dinghies with family members, including his wife and his son, Rod Johnstone finally had a 24-foot sloop, big enough for his growing young family to race and to enjoy sailing.

Ragtime looks every inch the racer. Although her designer and builder did not know it when she was launched, *Ragtime* would become the prototype for one of the most successful small keelboats in the world.

Rod thought of Sandy as his "sailmaking guru," and credits him with making several detail suggestions that were incorporated into *Ragtime*'s sail plan. In the spring of 1975, Rod ordered the rig and sails, and made a memorable family outing to the Stonington Foundry to cast the lead for the keel, with everyone helping. Then work came to an abrupt halt in June.

Rod explained: "I lost focus on the project because I ran out of funds. I had been hoping to get the boat ready in time for the 1975 MORC (Midget Ocean Racing Club) International Regatta, to be hosted by our yacht club in Stonington in September. Prospects were gloomy because I could not find anyone to put up the estimated $8,000 to pay for professional labor to finish building the boat. So the keel sat in front of the basketball net, waiting nearly a year for the boat to come out of the garage. Numerous other activities and distractions delayed the project until March 1976, when I laminated the mahogany rudder and spruce tiller."

The final fairing and finishing took place in April, and on May 1, 1976, a bright sunny day, Rod and John, supervised by

Libby, their mother, dragged the boat out into the sunshine.

"When we rolled the hull out of the garage the first time, it scratched the door jambs on each side," John said. "That's how tight it was."

A crowd of 25 family, friends, and neighbors gathered for a "hull-raising" party in the driveway. Between them, they lifted the surprisingly light hull above their heads and lowered it carefully onto the keel, which had been waiting in a cradle for months. Lucia then crawled underneath with a bucket of fiberglass and bonded the keel to the hull. The job of joining the hull and keel took a mere 25 minutes from start to finish. Rod noted that the ensuing party, with beer, soft drinks, and Lucia's spaghetti, lasted considerably longer.

The name *Ragtime* reflects Rod's love of music. He is an accomplished banjo player with a large repertoire of songs. Rod launched *Ragtime* under gray skies at the old Stonington Boat Works on Saturday, May 15, 1976. John well remembers launching day. He arrived in time to complete the final installation of the upper rudder gudgeons and to fit the rudder.

Typical of many amateur boat builders, Rod was slightly concerned that his boat might not float. Phil admitted to similar concerns. They need not have worried. *Ragtime* actually appeared to float high in the water, above her marks, until her builder realized it was low tide and the bottom of the keel was sitting on the mud. Towed into deeper water, she settled exactly on her lines, and to Rod's relief, she did not leak.

Phil told of being somewhat miffed initially because, after all his hard work, he was not invited out on *Ragtime*'s maiden sail. As it turned out, the day was very windy and he was happy to stay on shore. He missed the maiden voyage and had to defer to the adults for *Ragtime*'s first race; even so, he said, "All that summer I took part in about 90 percent of the races, because we spent the summer racing as a family."

Ragtime entered 21 races in the summer of 1976 and won all but two of them—in those she finished a respectable second and fourth. John said the first race, the Niantic Bay Early Bird, was the most eventful. He and Rod had sailed the 14 miles to the starting point at the Niantic Yacht Club the night before under main alone. Only one week since her launching, Rod had never hoisted the headsail on *Ragtime*. The race crew for the following morning consisted of Rod on the helm, plus Lucia, John, and Herb Holmwood.

"By the time we'd got the lines sorted out, we didn't get the genoa up until five minutes before the start," John remembered. That small element of confusion had little effect on the boat's performance. *Ragtime* kept pace with the fleet on the first leg, and took the lead on the second. The westerly wind climbed through 15 knots and up to 20 knots. Rounding the windward mark, bell number 8 off the Connecticut River, it was hazy and no other boats were in sight astern. Rod wanted to fly the spinnaker for the long downwind run, but John vehemently disagreed and won. At that point, they knew they had either gone to the wrong mark, or they were so far ahead that the spinnaker was unnecessary. Besides, the lifelines had not been installed, and John had no intention of going to the foredeck.

"We planed at speed down to the next mark at Bartlett's Reef. We were the smallest boat in our class," said John, "and we finished half an hour ahead of all other boats without setting a spinnaker."

Rod was understandably elated at his success. John referred to his brother's trademark "alligator" grin whenever he won a race. That saurian smile would have been well in evidence in the summer of 1976. *Ragtime* won her next four offshore races as well. No known boat of her size had ever sailed as fast. She consistently beat other—bigger—boats, many of which had been built for racing. Inevitably, she began to attract attention from other sailors—day sailors as well as racers.

After winning handily in his class on both days at the 1976 Spring Off Soundings Series at Block Island, Rhode Island, in June, with Lucia, John, and Phil aboard as crew, Rod stood with a group of sailors at "The Oar" on Block Island at the post-race party. "Legendary racing sailor Ed Raymond told me what a great-looking boat he thought *Ragtime* was," Rod recalled. "Ed had a keen eye for a good

The children in Rod and Lucia Johnstone's family enjoyed sailing in *Ragtime* and enhanced their own skills at her helm.

From left to right, John Johnstone (seated), Bob Johnstone (standing in cabin doorway), Rod Johnstone (standing on deck), and Lucia Johnstone (seated) before the start of a morning race.

sailboat, and was known to snarl occasionally about modern fiberglass 'rulebeaters' that resembled Clorox bottles. It suddenly dawned on me that I had something special, something marketable. My old dream of becoming a professional sailboat designer seemed achievable. That's when I first started thinking about how to put *Ragtime* into production."

The first thing Rod did after that weekend was contact his older brother. By then, Bob was marketing director for AMF/Alcort in Waterbury, Connecticut. Bob was in the boat business, and he wasn't far away.

"I called him up and invited him to join me for the next race on *Ragtime*, if he could stand crewing for his younger brother for the first time ever," Rod said. "I wanted to know what he thought of the boat, because he had never seen it."

Two weeks later, the three Johnstone brothers raced together on the same sailboat for the first time, off Groton Long Point. Lucia gamely joined them on *Ragtime* as a fourth crew member. Explaining his reasons for getting Bob on board, Rod said, "Bob was a career marketing man and had just entered the sailboat business the previous summer. So I valued his judgment highly."

Rod's core racing crew for the summer consisted of Lucia; his sons Jeff, Phil, and Alan; his brother John; and his nephew Clay Burkhalter. *Ragtime* rarely had the same crew aboard twice in a row. Fourteen members of Rod's immediate and extended family spanning three generations raced on *Ragtime*. They included Rod's mother, Libby; brother Bob; and his son Drake.

At summer's end, after steering *Ragtime* in a race for the first time, with Rod, Lucia, and

Bob's wife, Mary, as crew, Bob was suitably impressed. He recalled a discussion that took place later on the club lawn at Fishers Island. "Eddie Maxwell, who was a well-regarded sailor in the Mystic area, came up to us and said, 'Hey, Rod, how much do you want to sell that boat for?'"

Rod answered that the boat was not for sale, but the brief conversation had sparked a thought in Bob's business mind. He suggested Rod should consider turning *Ragtime* into a commercial product. Bob told him, "You've done a great job of designing it and now here's evidence that someone may want a copy." Later, Bob conducted market research that confirmed his view.

Rod referred to his boat as the "family magnet" because it brought the family together in many ways—not only his immediate family, but his extended family as well. He said, "*Ragtime* bridged the generation gap and caused different branches of the Johnstone clan to come back in close touch with one another after years of almost total separation."

Certainly, Jeff Johnstone, now president of J/Boats, recalls the stimulus of that summer as the race wins piled up. "I remember less about the winning and more about the excitement of exceeding expectation every week, competing against larger boats with older and more numerous crews. Our crew probably averaged about 14 to 15 years old (not counting Rod and Lucia), and we came from a small-boat dinghy experience, sailing Lasers, 420s, Bluejays, etc. An Ensign at 22 feet even seemed big back then. Rod did a great job, consciously or not, of lowering expectation, and I suppose the young crew helped create a natural 'underdog' feel to the program. As it turns out, *Ragtime* was an easy boat for 15-year-olds to handle, and in fact probably benefited more by having dinghy sailors aboard. There's no doubt that by summer's end we were no longer 'underdogs,' but in fact dominating most of the races. None of us knew at the time that sailing *Ragtime* would ever mean more than the summer Saturday races in Fishers Island Sound."

Drake Johnstone, Rod's nephew, was an assistant sailing instructor at the Wadawanuck Yacht Club in Stonington in 1976. He recalled sailing on *Ragtime* with Rod in a number of races. ". . . Whatever boats we raced against, nothing else came close to it [*Ragtime*] for speed," he said.

Libby Johnstone with her yacht-designer son, Rodney, sails *Ragtime*, the prototype for Rod's highly successful J/24, in the summer of 1976.

Ragtime's final race was in an early October howling northeaster. She planed on a spinnaker reach all the way back from Block Island at the end of a stormy weekend series. Rod said with pride, "That runaway downwind first-to-finish performance against everything up to 50 feet LOA was a fitting way for *Ragtime* to end its racing career."

Ragtime only raced for one season, but she had made her mark. If no boats of a similar size could keep up with *Ragtime*, the first J/24, the only alternative was to build more and develop a fleet, or fleets, of the boat and race against each other. Such a bold move required more than just a talented boat designer. It required a team: a team with vision. And a team, albeit a small one, was available.

Ragtime surprised sailboat racing fans in Connecticut and Rhode Island in the summer of 1976 by consistently winning events, sometimes against larger boats.

Two

A Synergistic Relationship

Rod Johnstone's monthly ad-selling trips to the Tillotson-Pearson factory during the years he worked for *Soundings* prompted him to call on Everett Pearson early in October 1976 for a different reason. Pearson said of that meeting, "Rod came to see me and told me about this new 24-foot sailboat he'd built, which was doing quite well at local races. At that time we were building the Etchells 22, so at first I was rather reluctant to build what appeared to be a competing boat."

Born in New York in 1933, Everett Pearson started building dinghies in a garage with his cousin, Clinton, while he was reading for a degree in economics at Rhode Island's prestigious Brown University in 1955. Within 18 months, they had graduated to 15-footers. In 1958, having moved the operation from a garage to an empty textile mill in Bristol, Rhode Island, they were contacted by Tom Potter from American Boat Building in East Greenwich. Potter wanted the cousins to build a 28-footer that would sleep four. That boat, designed by Carl Alberg, became the popular Pearson *Triton*, which sold about 800 hulls before production ceased.

Opposite page:
The J/24 is constructed from Lloyd's approved Baltek end-grained balsa core using hand–laid-up fiberglass in both hull and deck. The mast is of tapered, anodized aluminum with airfoil spreaders.

Left: Rod Johnstone designed and built a sailboat in his garage in the mid 1970s. Less than three decades later, more than 11,000 boats have been built from his designs, including 5,400 from that first successful model, the original J/24. **Center:** Bob Johnstone has an impressive résumé filled with marketing successes. He started J/Boats, Inc. with his brother Rodney in 1977. An avid and skilled racing sailor like his brother, Bob has owned a series of J boats. **Right:** Everett Pearson, known as the "grandfather of fiberglass boat building," has been actively involved in the production of the J/Boats, Inc. line of racers and cruiser/racers since day one.

Everett and Clinton soon had 500 people working for them building sailboats. For a time, the two entrepreneurs owned the old Herreshoff boat-building facilities in Bristol, Rhode Island. After selling a controlling interest to Grumman Allied Industries in 1961, Everett and Clinton eventually went their separate ways. Clinton left in 1964 to found Bristol Yachts, still in operation today. Everett stayed on with Grumman for another two years. When he left to go out on his own, he had to agree not to build boats for three years. He continued to work in fiberglass, but for industrial purposes only, until he could resume building boats. Everett teamed up with multi-millionaire Neil Tillotson in the late 1960s to form Tillotson-Pearson, Inc. (TPI). For Rod Johnstone, Everett Pearson was, without doubt, the best and most knowledgeable builder with whom to join forces.

After spending an hour aboard with Rod at the mooring in Stonington in early October 1976, Pearson agreed to produce *Ragtime*. Rod offered to take Everett out for a sail, but he declined because he had read reports about the boat's speed in the Providence *Journal*, and his wife, Ginny, was waiting in the car. Rod was sure Everett liked what he saw, especially the simplicity of the boat. "The clincher was, when we went ashore, Everett got Ginny to have a look at *Ragtime* and she expressed her approval. I was convinced then that we had a deal," Rod said.

Explaining his decision to accept the job, Pearson said, "The J/24 was smaller than the Etchells 22, so I felt they would not be competing designs."

Soon after, on October 16, 1976, Everett and Rod signed an agreement for TPI to produce *Ragtime* as the J/24. Rod would take care of the advertising and sales. According to Rod, he chose the designation J/24 to connote speed and simplicity. "Too many boats," he said, "were named after birds or beasts or fish, or natural phenomena. I wanted to keep the name anonymous so that the designation would not inhibit or influence sailors when naming their own boats. Also, J is the first letter of my last name."

Fleets of J/24s have been familiar sights at regattas worldwide since shortly after the first production J/24s rolled out of Everett Pearson's New England–based factory in 1977.

He was also well aware that the *J* designation lent itself as an effective reminder of the elegant fleet of fast J-Class boats that had competed for the America's Cup in years gone by. The favorable connotation could only be to the J/24's benefit. To promote the boat, and the concept, Rod and *Soundings*' production manager, Bill Morgan, had already created the *J* logo in the darkroom at *Soundings*.

Before Rod could haul her out of the water for the winter at the end of her first and only season of racing, *Ragtime* dragged her own mooring ashore at Wamphassuc Point in Stonington during a mid-October storm. She never sailed again. Still intact despite the storm's efforts, a crane hoisted her off the rocks and placed her on a flatbed trailer, which rolled her away to Tillotson-Pearson, Inc. Everett used the existing *Ragtime* hull as a plug to make the tooling for the J/24 line. In the course of construction, he made a few minor modifications, such as smoothing out the join where the cabin flowed into the deck. That made it easier to build and to pull the completed hull out of the mold. At the end of its useful life, *Ragtime*'s hull came to an ignominious end three years later, when it was cut up with a chainsaw and tossed into a dumpster.

"It made me cry," admitted Rod, "but using *Ragtime* to make production molds had destroyed it anyway. The production J/24s were built heavier and more durable, with balsa core covered with thicker fiberglass skins. Also, we did not want the old *Ragtime* out there sailing when we were trying to promote the J/24 as a strict one-design racing class—all boats completely alike."

The first of three full-page ads for the J/24, donated by Rod's boss, Jack Turner, appeared in the November 1976 issue of *Soundings*. The first few orders trickled in, some sight unseen, thanks to the ads in *Soundings*. Then the factory welcomed its first six visitors, all prospective owners from Lake Minnetonka, Minnesota. Among them was John Savage, who had been an usher at the wedding of Rod's parents in 1932. Savage soon owned one of the first J/24s. Another group of possible buyers came up from Hampton, Virginia. At this point, the hull and deck molds were still being fabricated. There was no finished boat to look at, not even an unfinished hull.

A few orders came in from Rod's friends and associates who had competed against *Ragtime* the previous summer, and Rod received his first

deposit check for a J/24 on January 9, 1977. It was time to make some serious decisions.

"Although I had many years of experience in the boat business and a wife who was ready, willing, and able to help me run a company, I knew J/Boats needed an immediate high level of marketing and sales expertise that neither Lucia nor I possessed at the time," Rod explained. Enter brother Bob.

Bob Johnstone has been racing sailboats since he was a tot. Although he does not remember the occasion, having to refer to tales handed down by others, Bob knows he raced with his father in the annual parent-child race in Stonington in the summer of 1936. It was not the most auspicious of beginnings for a future racer, although, to be fair, it has to be

Just about the only way to photograph a J/24 from dead ahead during a race downwind (or upwind) is from another J/24.

J/24 Principal Dimensions

LOA	24.0 feet
LWL	20.0 feet
Beam	8.9 feet
Draft	4.0 feet
Ballast	950 pounds
Displacement	3,100 pounds
Engine	4-horsepower outboard
100% SA	261.0 square feet
I	26.25 feet
J	9.5 feet
P	28.0 feet
E	9.75 feet
SA/Dspl	20
Displ/L	173

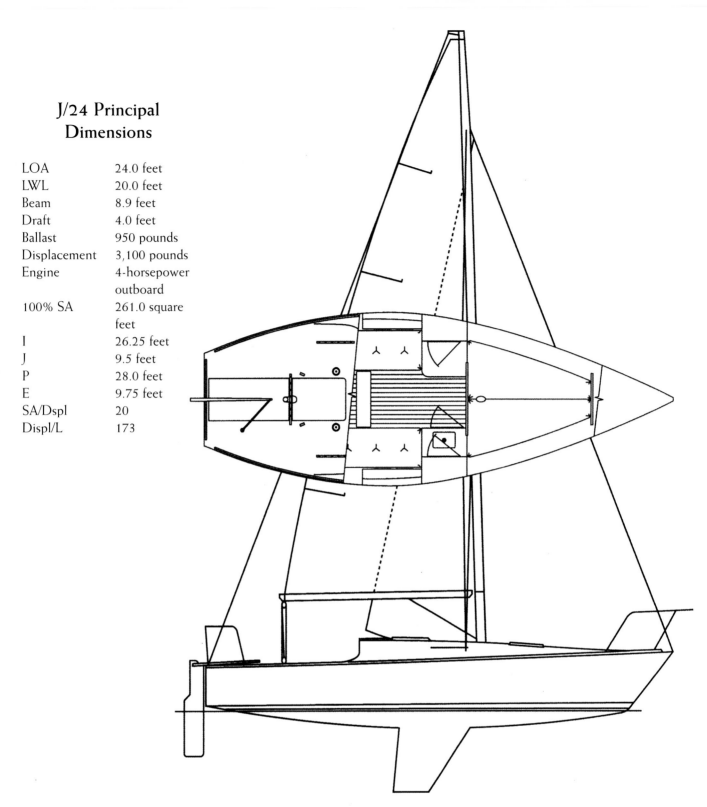

explained that he was only two years old at the time. Forbidden to touch the helm during the child's lap, Bob's father could only watch as his infant partner responded with a stubborn, "No!" to his orders and let go of the helm, thereby giving up the lead and losing the race.

Bob, like Rod and their father before them, is a Princeton graduate. He married his wife, Mary, a few days after leaving Princeton in 1956 and joined Quaker Oats in Cedar Rapids, Iowa, where Stuart, their first son, was born. Two years into his career, at 23, Quaker sent Bob (and the family) to its factory in Cali, Colombia, as plant manager. Another two years further on,

Bob had risen to CEO of the company's Colombian and Ecuadorian operations, with responsibility for some 300 employees. Two new family members came aboard when Drake and Helen were born in Cali. From Colombia, Bob transferred to neighboring Venezuela, where another son—Peter—joined the family.

The mountainous terrain where the Johnstones lived in Colombia had offered little opportunity for sailing, although Bob and Mary did sail a log canoe in the harbor at Santa Marta on one visit to the Pacific coast. The Venezuela posting was an improvement as far as sailing was concerned. Bob started a

Sunfish fleet at the Guataparo Country Club in Valencia and won the Venezuelan National Championship twice. He and Mary—and the children—sailed on lakes and on the Caribbean off magnificent beaches. From Venezuela, Quaker moved Bob back to the States, to Wilmette, Illinois.

Bob's sailing experience, like Rod's, is extensive. He and his family crew have won numerous racing trophies. He was secretary/treasurer of the U.S. Olympic Yachting Committee and a director of U.S. Sailing, as well as chairman of U.S. Sailing's One-Design Class Council and Industry Council.

After 17 years with Quaker Oats, where Bob was also product group manager of pet foods in the United States and Canada, Quaker's 1968 'Marketing Man of the Year,' and director of market strategy and analysis, he resigned in 1974 to start his own company. Utilizing the artistry of America's leading environmental photographers, he formed Naturescapes to produce photomurals of nature subjects. One year later, he joined AMF/Alcort, manufacturer of Sunfish and Paceship sailboats, as vice president of marketing. Mary then took over the running of Naturescapes, while Bob successfully turned

Rod Johnstone's intent was to design a boat that could beat other boats upwind as well as downwind. He achieved his goal with his first production boat, the J/24. It was awarded International Class status in 1981.

around the failing Sunfish brand to make the AMF Division profitable once more.

In 1976, after conducting intense product research, Bob tried, unsuccessfully, to interest his employers at AMF/Alcort to take on the project of building a shoal-draft trailerable sailboat similar to the J/24. At that time, Rod designed and arranged for a one-off J/23 sloop to be built as an entry for a design contest organized by Bob to determine what design AMF/Alcort would produce in 1977.

After sailing on *Ragtime* in the summer of 1976, Bob decided to include the J/24 in his market research and received positive feedback from prospective boat buyers. Bob offered great encouragement to Rod and started passing on valuable advice and marketing tips by telephone that fall.

By early 1977, with boats rolling down the production line, Rod's optimism was tempered by uncertainty about the future. He remembers being in a quandary about which direction J/Boats should take, and his notes from that time reflect his dilemma. Help, however, was close at hand. Sure of the new boat's potential in the marketplace, Bob resigned from AMF/Alcort at the end of January 1977. He went to see Rod in Stonington and suggested they form a partnership.

"The market research I had conducted gave me the courage to leave AMF and join forces with Rod," Bob said. "We had a boat that consumer research had shown was desired by 50 percent of the people thinking about buying a boat between 20 feet and 30 feet."

Rod, the company's vice president, secretary, and treasurer, invested his J/24 design and his creativity. He kept the books and focused on getting completed boats delivered. In his turn, Bob put up $20,000 to become equal partner with Rod and took on the role of company president and marketing expert. Half that financial investment went to pay the balance owed on the new prototype J/23, which never went into production. That prototype was sold a year later.

The brothers launched J/Boats, Inc. in February 1977, and Bob began to establish an international dealer network soon after.

Discussing the early days of J/Boats, Rod said: "Having a great builder like Everett Pearson was not enough. It was only after Bob quit his real job at AMF/Alcort and became my partner in February 1977 that we began to sell J/24s by the hundreds. Bob knew how to think big in order to market and sell boats, and he is a real deal-closer to boot. It was just what the fledgling company needed to have any hope of being really successful. I was

Synchronized port and starboard, a pair of J/24s with red and green hulls, respectively, stand at anchor in a cove off Narragansett Bay, Rhode Island. The red boat, *Top of the World*, belonged to Bob Johnstone.

The International J/24 Class Association, which has reduced its scries to 10 countries, oversees the J/24 World Championship races. Continental championships are held in North America, South America, and Europe. In addition, there are many regional events, such as this race off the New England coast.

thrilled to have Bob as a partner, and suddenly excited about future prospects. The timing could not have been scripted better."

In fact, it wasn't quite that easy, although the first two production J/24s arrived at the Boston and Hartford boat shows for their first public showing that weekend. For the first few weeks, little happened. Bob said: "I sent Stuart up to Marblehead, Massachusetts, to live on my boat for a couple of weeks to see if he could sell a boat or two. He took a few people out sailing but there were no takers."

Bob and Rod really believed people in boating-renowned places such as Marblehead and Newport would jump at the chance of a good new design, but it didn't happen—at least, not as quickly as the brothers expected.

"It's amazing how reactionary people are about new designs in the sailing world," Bob said. "Actually, I think we sold a couple

of boats in the Narragansett Bay area, that's all."

Tillotson-Pearson built the first J/24s in an old textile mill at Fall River in Massachusetts. Rod supplied the design and *Ragtime* as a model; Tillotson-Pearson paid for the tooling and production line. Over the course of their business arrangement, Bob said Everett Pearson became like another brother.

As Bob built up his nationwide network of dealers, some interesting requests for special orders came in. One dealer sent in an order for a boat in bright colors: international orange hull and deck with yellow nonskid. Bob was understandably reluctant to accept the order as it was. He told the dealer, "I want full payment up front for this one because if the customer defaults, I'm stuck with a colorful boat I can't sell." He changed his mind when the dealer explained that the customer's name

Whenever two or more J/24s meet on the water, a race is inevitable. In 1995, the design was elected to the American Sailboat Hall of Fame.

Nearly three decades after the first production J/24 was launched, the design is still in production in Argentina, Italy, and the United States. Twenty to 25 hulls come off the production lines each year.

was Ronald McDonald. The colors, of course, represented those of the McDonald chain of fast-food outlets.

Bob's strategy for setting up his sales outlets is an effective one. All J/Boats dealers own a J themselves. "If the dealer is excited about a new product and owns one for his personal use, loyal customers are likely to follow suit," Bob said.

Sales may have been slow to start, but after the summer racing season and a string of successes for the J/24, they picked up in the

fall of 1977. Suddenly, the J/24 took off. In a few months, sailors in Texas alone ordered 150 J/24s.

When Bob joined Rod as his partner, neither of them dreamed what the future would hold, and how that family business would burgeon and gradually embrace more and more family members. Rod's self-styled family "magnet" became the catalyst for a family business, and it was all due to *Ragtime*, a would-be yacht designer's initial success. Rod, however, credits Bob with being the key to the early marketing

"A barn door and a bedsheet can go downwind. I wanted a boat that would beat other boats upwind," says Rod Johnstone. The result was the by-now ubiquitous J/24.

Opposite: A J/24 seen from the air. Wherever it sails, a J/24 is usually out in front of the fleet. Hull number 5000 was launched in 1992, and the J/24 continues to sell.

and sales success. Although highly competitive, and both strong-willed, there is no doubt that together Rod and Bob are a formidable team. The addition of Everett Pearson made for a near-perfect business triangle that was almost impossible to beat.

Mention a J/24 to Rod and a proud smile lights up his face. He says, "In many ways it is still my favorite of all my designs, especially because so many people have had so much fun sailing it."

Bob, too, has his reflective moments. Speaking about a vacation in Portofino, Italy, he said: "I woke up one morning to see the small harbor crowded with J/24s. The Italians have a wonderful flare for design. . . . For them to appreciate this one the way they have, well, it's just very gratifying."

Rod Johnstone designed the J/30 in 1977. J/Boats built a prototype in 1978 and began production on the model before the end of the year. The first hull came off the line in January 1979.

Three

The Incomparable J/24

"Remember sailing a J/24 for the first time? The boat seemed to defy gravity, or at least friction, as it surfed down waves in perfect control, blowing by 35-footers in the process." John Kretschmer, noted sailing authority and international delivery skipper, reminisced about the J/24 while reviewing a much later and larger J model in April 1999. Kretschmer's feelings about the J/24 appear to be universal. Anyone who has ever experienced sailing on Rod Johnstone's first successful design makes similarly complimentary comments.

Opposite page:
J/24 Class racing is an extremely competitive sport. Speed differences between the top boats and crews can be little more than the difference in rig tuning.

The J/24's cockpit and deck layout are designed for minimum clutter and maximum efficiency.

"The world's most-popular one-design keelboat." The J/24's clean lines, relatively small hull-wetted area, and fin keel can be seen to advantage out of the water and supported on a cradle.

Opposite page: A pair of J/24s runs downwind with spinnakers set. There are countless stories of the greyhound-like performance J/24s show in competition with each other and against larger boats.

The annals of the International J/24 Class Association are an excellent measure of the worldwide popularity of the impressive 24-footer. Since the first "Worlds," which appropriately took place at Newport, Rhode Island, in the summer of 1979, the annual event has spanned the globe. Twelve countries have hosted the race series in the more than two and a half decades since, some of them more than once. In addition, 15 countries have their own J/24 associations. As Jeff Johnstone, now president of J/Boats, Inc., likes to remind people, by late 2004 there were some 5,300 J/24s sailing throughout the world—an impressive number by any standard. Advertising for the J/24 lists the class, quite brazenly, as "the world's most-popular one-design keelboat, selected for the ISAF Nations

Whenever two J/24s meet on the sea, or on a lake, it's a good excuse for a race. The spirit of competition between owners can be intense. *Sweet Reason* in close maneuvers with a competitor.

Family members of all ages enjoy racing J/24s. As Rod Johnstone said, "It's a family boat." It's also an excellent boat in which to learn and practice racing skills.

Cup and the choice of sailing fun by more than 50,000 sailors of all ages." So, how did this home-designed little boat achieve such international renown?

It really started with *Ragtime*'s phenomenally successful first season of racing in 1976. Those wins, coupled with early advertising brochures, prompted a small group of Minnesota sailors from the Wayzata Yacht Club on Lake Minnetonka to take a good look at the J/24. They obviously liked what they saw. Two of them, John Gjerde and Rolf Turnquist, formed a partnership and placed an order for their boat in January 1977. They took hull number 7, which was the second boat out of the factory. By March, the Minnesota group

had ordered five out of the initial 25 J/24s produced. The Wayzata Yacht Club sailors, with justification, pride themselves on being J/24 fleet number 1. They were not the only ones to see the potential in the new boat. A slow but steady stream of orders began to flow in.

The first TPI-built J/24, a bright red hull number 3 called *Red Pepper*, was launched at Stonington on March 1, 1977. With a J/24 finally sailing, orders began to increase. As a new series-produced "stock" boat, the J/24 still had to prove itself on the race course to a wide audience. It did that quite emphatically. It didn't seem to matter what handicap formula was employed or where the boat was being raced: J/24s won.

A fleet of J/24s with spinnakers flying begins the downwind leg of a race in light airs.

Rod and Bob took the helms of the first two production J/24s in the two largest 1977 MORC events on Long Island Sound. They were the 100-mile race around Faulkner Island from Larchmont Yacht Club in May and the Block Island Race Week in June. They finished one and two at both events, with Rod winning the first and Bob the second. Rod's crew for the grueling light-air overnight race (around Faulkner Island) was his brother John, plus sailmaker Sandy Van Zandt and his wife, Sidney.

"We were, of course, sailing with a full suit of Van Zandt Sails," said Sandy, "and [our boat] bested all the other J/24s, but most importantly, Rod's older brother and lifelong sailing rival, Bob."

For Block Island, Jeff replaced John in Rod's crew, while Bob exacted his revenge with his sons Stuart and Drake aboard, as well as sailmaker Dave Curtis.

In September, the brothers organized a fleet of 13 J/24s, which dominated their class at the MORC International Regatta in Annapolis, Maryland, with their performance and dominated the event with their numbers.

Drake Johnstone, second son of Bob Johnstone, recalled racing on his father's J/24 on Long Island Sound in the summer of 1977. In heavy seas coming up to and rounding the weather mark, with a Cal 40 close by, one of the crew asked Bob if they should put up the spinnaker. Bob looked at Drake, then 18 years old, who grinned back and said, "Sure. Let's do it." With the chute up, the J/24 covered the 10 miles downwind to the finish in 40 minutes, beating many larger boats, some up to 40 feet. "The J/24 was head and shoulders above other boats in its size and range," Drake noted.

Famed small-boat sailor and author John Rousmaniere joined Bob Johnstone in *Top of*

The clean and user-friendly deck of the J/24. Rod Johnstone laid down a strict set of one-design class rules for the J/24, including having the boat weighed—in stripped condition—before a race.

Opposite page: "It was like selling shoes," said Bob Johnstone. "…I'll take a red one. I'll take a green one. I'll take a black one, and so on." A trio of colorful J/24 hulls sails neck and neck.

Opposite page: Rod and Jeff Johnstone, and a substantial crew, raced 19 other J/24s in green-hulled *Chameleon* in the first J/24 one-design event off Key West, Florida, early in 1978.

the World for a race at Groton Long Point, Connecticut. Only three of the 14 entries were J/24s, and they were the bottom-rated boats. Rousmaniere wrote, "After 15 miles of predominantly light-air reaching, we were the first boat to finish—by 4 1/2 minutes." Rod Johnstone's J/24 came home second.

Each successive win became a banner advertisement for the J/24. At the end of summer, with a string of wins to its credit, J/24 sales took off.

"It was like selling shoes," said Bob. "You know: I'll take a red one. I'll take a green one. I'll take a black one, and so on."

Hoping for sales of 250 boats in the first year, the new company passed and then tripled its target. With the revolutionary racer gaining quickly in popularity and constantly beating the competition, J/24 owners began racing each other, and a new one-design class came into being.

J/24 One-Design

The first J/24 one-design racing event took place off Key West, Florida, early in 1978.

Twenty boats entered the competition, which was won by Mark Ploch of Clearwater, Florida, and his crew in *Tchau*. A few months later, 68 J/24s entered the first North American Championship at Newport, Rhode Island, where Charlie Scott from Annapolis, Maryland, steered *Smiles* to victory.

Determined to avoid the pitfalls of other one-design classes, where supposedly identical boats are actually quite different, the Johnstones laid down a strict set of one-design class rules for the J/24. The centerpiece of the rules was the stipulation that, unless specifically permitted by the rules, all modifications were prohibited. The rules covered all speed-producing factors, including measurement of the mast, sails, keel, rudder, equipment weight, and, eventually, crew and boat weight.

According to J/Boats, Inc. history, 1,000 J/24s were ready for action by the end of 1978. In addition, the company had signed agreements with builders in Argentina, Brazil, Australia, California, and the United Kingdom, where a British yachting journalist with a keen sense of humor referred to the J/24 as a "Laser with a lid."

A tightly packed fleet of J/24s rounds a mark during a one-design race. Racing is all about strategy, tactics, and speed. Successful J boat racers understand the need for all three. They are dedicated to winning, and J boats have the necessary speed. In a one-design race, strategy and tactics can mean the difference between winning and losing.

Sailmaker Mark Ploch duplicated his 1978 Mid-Winters success at Key West in January 1979 when he finished first overall out of a fleet of 51 boats. Charlie Scott, winner of the 1978 North American Championship, took second place. The summer of 1979 heralded the first J/24 World Championship. Seventy-eight boats entered, most from the United States. In fact, only seven foreign boats took part; they came from Australia, Canada, Sweden, and the Virgin Islands. Held on Rhode Island Sound off Newport, Rhode Island, over five increasingly windy days in August, the final race of 25 miles tested everyone's mettle. The course ran from the starting line off Castle Hill, south to Brenton Reef tower, and then around Conanicut Island and back. With a southerly wind pushing 35 knots and waves building up in excess of 4 feet, a number of boats broached and about 10 capsized—among them, the Johnstone brothers, Rod and Bob. The crews righted all boats again in double-quick time, without getting

the cabin interiors wet. In spite of the extreme conditions and a few frights for many, all boats and crews survived the race series. Charlie Scott emulated his North American Championship win by taking the honors again in *Smiles*.

The North American Championship that year went to Corpus Christi, Texas, where Mark Ploch and *Tchau* again proved successful. Conditions at Corpus Christi failed to match the wild week at Newport, yet the seven-race series kept the crews busy. Early in the week, under overcast skies, a southeast breeze varied from 10 to 15 knots. As the week progressed, the skies cleared and the wind all but doubled to 20 to 25 knots. As a result, the shallow waters of Corpus Christi Bay developed steep waves, up to 5 feet high, causing the fleet to take white water over the bows while racing upwind. Bob, Stuart, Drake, and Rod Johnstone, sailing Bob's bright-red hull number 653, *Top of the World*, came in third overall with Olympic silver medalist John Kolius close behind. One morning during the regatta, Mark Ploch found

himself the butt of Texas humor. He arrived at his boat to find it all but buried under a stack of hay about 5 feet high. Rumor suggested Mark Foster, another J/24 racer in the same event, had something to do with the joke.

Not content with competing against almost identical boats in one-design races, J/24 owners continued to win other races, often against larger boats. And the orders kept coming in. TPI Composites rolled hull number 2000 out of the factory in 1979. Each year brought more successes for J/24s, and a new builder joined the J/Boats family.

Nissan Motors, in Japan, began production of J/24s in 1980. Nissan would eventually sell in excess of 200 of the model. Also in 1980, a J/24 won the Caribbean Ocean Racing Circuit, the design became an official International Yacht Racing Union (IYRU) International Class, and *SAIL* magazine gave advertising a huge boost by naming the J/24 the "best keelboat in 30 years." The second annual J/24 Worlds went to the Mediterranean, where the northern Italian

city of San Remo hosted the event. John Kolius from Texas steered *San Brandano* to victory in the J/24's first foreign setting. The North American Championship that year took place on the demanding waters of San Francisco Bay, where Middletown, Rhode Island, racer Ed Adams won in *Shazamm*. By the end of 1980, it had become obvious that the J/24 was the ideal keelboat for "'round the buoys" racing.

Forty boats took part in the 1981 Worlds in Sydney, Australia, with the host country fielding 21 entries. Other boats came from Britain, Ireland, Japan, Italy, the United States, and New Zealand. Local boy Mark Bethwaite won in *Bandit*, a boat he had borrowed from Bunker Snyder III, an American visitor who joined the crew for the competition. In the seven races of the series, Bethwaite and his crew won three—the first win coming in the third race when *Bandit* passed American Dave Curtis' boat on the second windward leg and maintained her position to the line. Two of the seven races took place on Sydney Harbour,

The Golden Gate Bridge and San Francisco Bay, with the city in the background. In 1980, the J/24 One-Design Class North American Championship races took place in this glorious setting.

one of which was a 20-mile distance race. The other five races were sailed offshore on the ocean. American boats finished second and third overall.

The June 1981 edition of *SAIL* magazine carried a two-page advertisement for J/Boats. Headed "Juniors of the World Unite!" it was subtitled, "(or, why the J/24 is the right boat for you)." Apparently aimed at the younger generation, their parents, and/or local yacht clubs, the advertisement carried a powerful and attractive message. A couple of lines stand out: "With main alone a 12-year-old can get through a line squall, aim the boat for home, and get there. . . . If you have confidence in a junior's judgment and sailing ability, you can turn them loose in a J/24 and let them sail out of sight."

International Championships
France hosted the first European Championship at La Trinité in 1982, and the magnificent city of Buenos Aires, Argentina, acted as a backdrop to the first South American Championship, held one year later. That event, with the course marked out on the historic Rio de la Plata estuary, gave Argentinian Alejandro Irigoyen at the helm of *Shawdow* his first J/24 win. Irigoyen and *Shawdow* won again in Buenos Aires in 1989, on Chile's Lake Rapel in 1990, and at Ancón, Peru in 1991.

An American Legend
Racing legend Ken Read recalled his first sail in a J/24. "It was while I was still in high school (in 1978). I was a sailing instructor at the time at the Barrington Yacht Club. A local club sailor named Dr. Richard Carleton of Barrington, Rhode Island, bought a J/24. It was the first of many to show up in Barrington."

Dr. Carleton recruited Read and others his age to be his crew, and they were happy to oblige. After that, Read and his friends talked constantly about sailing J/24s.

"That [J/24] was the coolest boat in town. It was a blast, and it was bright yellow!" Read said.

By 1983, Ken Read had graduated from Boston University and started working for sailmaker Bill Shore. "My job was to sell sails

Opposite page: Racing downwind, side by side with an identical boat, squeezing every ounce of speed out of the boat with spinnaker and main keeps crews busy. Two J/24s fight for position.

and win races in J/24s," he said. "The more races we won, the more sails we sold."

About that time, Everett Pearson, a great family friend, told Ken about a "junker J/24" in his boatyard that had been accidentally dropped off a hoist in Annapolis. Ken scraped up as much money as he could, then in partnership with his bosses, Bill and Doug Shore, he bought the boat and fixed her up. Ken named her *Maggie*, his mother's nickname as a girl, and sailed her hard. That summer, Ken Read discovered the J/24's performance could be further enhanced with some radical rig tuning, both in light and heavy air.

Whether racing or weekend cruising from one cove to the next, the more than 5,000 fractional-rigged J/24s that have been built in a variety of countries are enjoyed by up to 50,000 sailors around the world.

The harbor at Monte Carlo, in the Principality of Monaco, is a popular haven for the boats of the rich and famous. Italian Luca Santella won the 1993 J/24 European Championship at Monte Carlo in *Jadine*.

A former college sailing champion, Rhode Islander Ken Read was six-time world champion in the J/24 Class. The vice president of North Sails, he continues to race and win races in a variety of boats.

"Everyone else at the time raced with a tighter headstay in light airs and probably not quite as tight as we did in heavy airs," he said. Read proved his theories in 1984 with a win on Lake Ontario in the North American Championship at Kingston, Ontario, and consolidated with a second North American win at Marion, Massachusetts, the next summer.

Although he has been credited with figuring out that the J/24's performance could be improved with radical tuning changes, particularly the use of forestay sag, Ken insists some improvements were discovered by accident.

"The shrouds spun open by mistake during a race at the Buzzards Bay Regatta in the summer of 1983," he explained, "and we ended up with a ton of sag in the forestay by the end of the race in about 4 knots of breeze."

With the forestay sag, *Maggie* just kept increasing her lead. "We didn't figure out that the shrouds weren't pinned until we got in to the dock at day's end," he said. "It was funny. We were about three [turns of the] threads away from the mast falling down!"

Having made the discovery, inadvertently though it may have been, Ken Read made good use of the knowledge. He and his crew experimented with the rigging nearly every time they went out. "If a little bit of sag worked," he argued, "why not try a lot?" He did try more sag, and it worked. The J/24 responded with characteristic agility and greater speed. Read and his crew continued to experiment with the rig and continued to win.

Beating upwind in
light airs, two J/24s
cross on opposite tacks.

Ken Read won his third
J/24 Class Association
World Championship at
Athens, Greece, in 1991,
under the shadow of
ancient buildings from
Greek history, such as
the Olympian Temple of
Zeus and the Parthenon.

The Dutch are great sailors and enjoy watching sailboat races. The 1993 J/24 Class Association European Championship was held at Medemblik on the Ijsselmeer.

out how to do that from time to time. The 1984 Worlds in Poole Bay [England] was proof of that. We snatched defeat from the jaws of victory with just one silly mistake. That regatta still haunts me."

While at Boston University, Ken Read had won the 1981–1982 Morris Trophy, awarded to the nation's outstanding collegiate sailor. By the time he graduated, he had a string of first- and second-place finishes in national and regional sailing events. He would go on to expand his expertise with an impressive series of wins in J/24s, including the North American Championship again in 1991 at Toronto, and in 1993 at Hampton, Virginia. Read also won the U.S. Mid-Winter Championship at Miami in 1993. He added the Rolex Yachtsman of the Year award to his collection of trophies in 1985 and again in 1995.

Overseas, Francesco de Angelis won the Worlds in *Le Coq Hardi* in 1987 at Capri, Italy, only the second non-American to win the annual event in the first nine years of the championships. An Italian won on home ground again in 1999, when Vasco Vascotto led the fleet across the line off Genoa. In 2001, Japan had its second stint at hosting the event, this time at Nishinomiya City on Osaka Bay. Local star Kazuyuki Hyodo took the line honors with *Sled*. At the 2003 Worlds, held off Medemblik, Holland, on the Ijsselmeer (aka Zuider Zee), an inland sea, an Italian won for a third time when Lorenzo Bressani took *Kaster* to victory.

Of the 26 J/24 World Championship held since 1979, with international entries increasing, American crews have won all but five events. Multiple wins have gone to John Kolius, who has two, and the Read brothers of Rhode Island have taken eight between them. Ken Read holds an impressive six wins in five countries, and younger brother Brad has two victories to his credit, so far. Ken said of his win on Atsumi Bay in Japan, "That was the best regatta of my life. For [us] five young guys, the whole experience was incredible. Not just the win. It was the fireworks displays. The signing autographs, the being put on a pedestal. It was really more than we were worth."

He graciously conceded that he and *Maggie's* crew were not alone in their discovery.

"I do think that Dave Curtis and a few others were also onto the sag though, maybe a bit more scientifically than we figured it out. I think our big advantage back then was really in the breeze. We were definitely one of the first to crank on our lower shrouds to get fairly radical headstay tension, sometimes coming back in to the dock with about 2 inches of inversion in the rig once we let off the backstay."

With a philosophical afterthought, Ken added, "There was a while there that the only way [for us] to lose a heavy air race was to beat ourselves, and we were young enough to figure

Opposite page: John Kretschmer wrote of the J/24, "The boat seemed to defy gravity, or at least friction, as it surfed down waves in perfect control . . . ." Whether the J/24 is surfing down waves or running downwind in choppy seas, competent crews can easily handle it.

Running downwind with spinnaker flying, in choppy and blustery conditions, this J/24 has a good edge over the following boat. In J/24 Class events, boats often have to fight hard to stay inches ahead of the competition.

Ken and his team had come close to winning the year before on a cold November week at Poole, on England's Dorset coast. "We were just too young and inexperienced," he said, "but we learned from it and won the next year."

Heidi Backus and her sisters won their first Rolex International Women's Keelboat Championship in a J/24 in 1985, and Backus joined Ken Read by winning the Rolex Yachtswoman of the Year award, also in 1985.

Winning races may have been at the forefront of Rod Johnstone's mind when he designed the J/24, but perhaps the true appeal of J/24s can best be explained by borrowing a few lines from the appropriate pages of the

J/24 crews tidy up their boats after a long and tiring day of racing.

Sailing close-hauled in a good breeze—the J/24's helmsman and crew have their weight positioned well over on the windward side to use their righting power effectively.

The Needles jut into the English Channel from the west end of the Isle of Wight. They are a familiar sight to participants in races out of the legendary town of Cowes, where the 1988 J/24 European Championship was held.

Opposite: Two J/24s cross on opposite tacks as they beat to the windward mark.

J/Boats website: "J/24 is for everyone, age 12 to 80, no matter what their style—racing, day sailing, or cruising. Her flared topsides make her dry on deck. Her 'weekender' cabin makes it possible to get warm on cold days, and she can be sailed easily by one person with only the mainsail." Add four words and the explanation is complete: "And she is fast."

In 1992, 16 years after *Ragtime*'s hull first settled into salt water in May 1976, the number of J/24s in the world had reached 5,000. Also in 1992, *Sailing World*'s Hall of Fame elected Rod Johnstone to its distinguished rolls. Three years later, his J/24 was equally honored with election to the American Sailboat Hall of Fame.

Since those heady days, the unstoppable J/24 has gone from success to more success. J/Boats, Inc. celebrated the J/24's silver anniversary with a regatta in Newport in 2003. Jeff Johnstone said the anniversary included a "who's who" one-day regatta of former J/24 champions, followed by a weekend "reunion," including a special showing by hull number 2 and hull number 7—two of the first boats built. The one-day "who's who" regatta

included Bob Johnstone with an all-family crew; Rod Johnstone, also with an all-family crew; former world champions Ken Read, Brad Read, Dave Curtis, Terry Hutchinson, Chris Larsen, and Bill Fortenberry; Pat Connerney, winner of the 1999 Rolex International Women's Keelboat Championship; Don Trask, West Coast J/Boat builder; famed Laser sailor and author Dick Tillman; and John Gjerde and Rolf Turnquist, the original partners in J/24 hull number 7, OZ, who now own J/24 hull number 3577.

Now in its 29th year, the J/24 is still in production in Argentina, Italy, and the United States, with about 20 to 25 boats coming off the lines each year. There are currently more than 5,300 J/24s sailing in 150 fleets in 40 countries.

The 2004 Worlds, held at Noroton Yacht Club in Darien, Connecticut, almost ended in true storybook fashion when Rod and Jeff Johnstone, sailing together on the 25th anniversary of the first Worlds, sailed to a tie with Jens Hookasen of Newport, Rhode Island. Hookasen won the 74-boat regatta in a tie-breaker.

Four

New Models for the 1980s

ollowing *Ragtime*'s phenomenal early racing successes and the beginning of production of the J/24, in the fall of 1977 Rod Johnstone started drawing the lines for a larger boat to serve a broader market. Bob Johnstone wrote, "Distinct from the J/24, the new boat would be primarily focused at the cruising market while carrying forward some of the J/24 features, such as fractional rig and performance-oriented design.

"At that point," explained Bob, "we were interacting with our potential buyers and the J/30 came about because enough people said they liked the concept of the J/24 and its performance, but they wanted a larger boat, one big enough to take the family cruising for a month if necessary. After half a dozen people asked us when we were going to come out with a 30-footer they could stand up in, we got the message and decided to move forward."

Opposite page:
The J/30, Rod Johnstone's second design produced by J/Boats, Inc., also carries a fractional rig. At 29.83 feet LOA and 25 feet LWL, the J/30 remained in production from 1979 to 1986, with 550 hulls built.

J/30 fleets can be found
on the U.S. East and
West coasts, as well as
in the Gulf and on the
Great lakes. The most
active fleet, with 50
boats, resides on
Chesapeake Bay.

After successfully testing a cold-molded wooden prototype in the summer of 1978, production began in December. J/Boats introduced the company's second offering early in 1979, when TPI launched J/30 hull number 1. In October 1978, Rod flew to Grand Rapids, Michigan, for a party at the home of Jim Stuursma, first J/30 class president, where six buyers ordered J/30 fleet number 1 to be home-ported at Macatawa Bay Yacht Club in Holland, Michigan.

"It was amazing how enthusiastic they were about the boat," said Rod, "even though we did not yet have any decent drawings or pictures of it. What sold them was the promise of a big J/24 that you could live on for the summer with the family, race one-design, and cruise all over Lake Michigan. They did all of the above when they got their boats the next summer."

They were enthusiastic, but, apparently, not completely sold. The same group showed up in Florida to check out the performance of the first J/30 in a race. Christened *Warwhoop*, the J/30 soon proved her pedigree as an ocean greyhound in the 1979 Southern Ocean Racing Conference (SORC). Famed racing skipper John Kolius was at the helm, with Rod on board among the crew to see how his latest design would hold up in what turned out to be one of the nastiest February Gulf Stream weather patterns in the long history of the event.

"We were the smallest boat in the whole fleet and our Michigan fleet members could not have been impressed, as we were the last boat in the last class to sail out under the Tampa Bay Bridge, going downwind in light air at the start of the 470-mile St. Pete to Ft. Lauderdale race," said Rod. "Fortunately, a severe weather front came through, so when we showed up at the Lauderdale Yacht Club two days later, we were the first boat in our class to finish, beside Ted Hood's 36-foot *Robin*. It was a rough ride—perfect J/30 weather—and nothing broke."

The J/30 was primarily focused at the cruising market but proved itself as a racer too. One survived the disastrous Fastnet Race of 1979 and carried its crew home to safety.

The J/30 is a cruiser/racer, able to enter long-distance races while accommodating a full crew comfortably overnight and offering the cooking and dining comforts of a larger boat.

Hull number 1 of the J/36 line. *Jazz* was Rod Johnstone's personal boat. The J/36 was not designed for grand prix racing. It was a cruiser with racing capability.

Rod added: "John Kolius is a great racing skipper and had a great crew on *Warwhoop*. Thanks to their superior seamanship in difficult conditions, no J/30 orders were canceled on that trip."

Kolius would go on to race in one of *Warwhoop*'s smaller sisters when he won the J/24 World Championship in San Remo, Italy, in 1980. He repeated the feat on San Francisco Bay in 1982.

Considerably larger and more comfortable than the J/24, at 29.83 feet LOA and 25 feet on the water line, the J/30 efficiently handles the dual roles of family cruising and racing with style. Equipped with a handcrafted wooden interior, standing head room for a crew, a reasonably spacious dining area and galley, a head, and a 15-horsepower inboard diesel for auxiliary power, the J/30 sports a large cruising cockpit able to accommodate three to four people on each side.

Maine residents Tom and Jane Babbitt owned a 28-foot ocean-going keelboat for a couple of years, but Tom got tired of seeing J/24s pass him with no apparent effort. That

element of frustration made Babbitt a prime candidate for ownership of a J boat.

"I like to cruise and I like to race. I like to win too," Tom said. In 1981, he sold the 28-footer and shifted his allegiance to J/Boats by purchasing a J/30. "Finally," he laughed, "I had a boat I could beat a J/24 with."

At an on-the-water racing seminar in Massachusetts, Rod Johnstone joined Babbitt and his crew on the J/30 and gave them an impromptu lesson in sailboat handling. Rod sat on the windward side with his long legs dangling over the water and his eyes fixed on the horizon. Without changing his position, he ordered Tom and crew to make a series of small sail adjustments. When they were completed, Rod pronounced his satisfaction. Intrigued, Tom questioned him about his decisions, as Rod had not once looked up at the sails, either before issuing the orders or after. Rod replied with a boat designer's classic one-liner, "She was making too much noise through the water."

As the number of J/30s climbed, Tom and Jane Babbitt ran the J/30 Class Association for several years but found the job too

The J/22 was intended as a one-design right from the start, and to meet dealer requests for a boat that would sell for under $10,000— where the J/24 used to be. By the time the J/22 arrived, the J/24's price had risen to $15,000.

The cabin interior on a J/36 reflects the superior craftsmanship that goes into all J boats from start to finish. The light woodwork is stylish and gives the cabin a feeling of extra space.

Boat 22, *Bretwalda*; Boat 28, *Top Gun*; and Boat 2, *Bozo's Circus* approach the windward mark for a spinnaker hoist during the 2003 J/35 North American Championship, hosted by the Etobicoke Yacht Club on Lake Ontario.

time-consuming. To get themselves out of the position, they sold their J/30 and moved up to a J/35, which had been introduced in the spring of 1983.

Close to 550 J/30s took to the water between 1979 and 1986, when production on the model halted. As a result, the type became one of North America's largest one-design classes over 24 feet. One J/30 entered the disastrous Fastnet Race of 1979. With

skipper Andy Cassel at the helm and crewmember Tim Levett, *Juggernaut* survived a couple of knockdowns and had to run under a bare pole for roughly 14 hours. She weathered the storm and reached port with crew intact. The Fastnet Race takes place in odd-numbered years on a roughly 618-mile course from Cowes, on the Isle of Wight off England's south coast, around the Fastnet Rock southwest of Ireland, and back to Plymouth, in

Devon. Participants and observers consider it one of the toughest ocean races of all. During the 1979 race, when winds reached Force 10 and mountainous seas broke over the fleet of 303 boats, 15 sailors died and five boats succumbed to the storm.

Although not competing in the Fastnet Race, another J/30 experienced the same vicious conditions. The storm, which some sailors referred to as "a great fury," caught up with Bill Wallace as he sailed out of the North Atlantic and into the English Channel. On a single-handed delivery passage from Bermuda to England, Wallace suffered a knockdown, but his boat came upright again and he reached port unaided. He later told Rod that the only problem he had during the knockdown was in getting himself nicked on the head by an unsecured coffee pot. Unrelated to the Fastnet Race tragedy but certainly noteworthy, a used-boat review in a magazine summed up the strengths of the J/30 design by noting ". . . J/30 is a tough boat to beat."

"The J/29 was the 'quick-fix' MORC racer," said designer Rod Johnstone. It was, in essence, a J/30 sawed off at the top. As a racer, it was hard to beat. A quartet of J/29s finished first, second, third, and fourth at Block Island (Rhode Island) Race Week.

Cruiser/Racers

The 1980s, the first full decade of J/Boats, Inc.'s existence, heralded 14 new boat designs. Of those, the J/41 and J/34 were considered race-only designs, both being designed to compete under the International Offshore

The fleet beats to windward during the 2003 J/35 North American Championship with Toronto's skyline in the background, dominated by the needle-like CN Tower.

Rule (IOR) —the grand prix racing rule at the time. The J/22 was intended as a one-design from day one to meet dealer requests for a boat that would sell for under $10,000; but in keeping with its predecessor, the J/24, it was designed as a recreational day sailer as well as a racer. Three of the remaining 11, the J/27, J/29, and J/33, leaned more toward racing. Jeff Johnstone said, "I'd call them 80 percent race/day sail and 20 percent cruise." The final eight boats introduced in the 1980s fall into the combined cruiser/racer category, although the J/37c and J/34c are classified as cruising boats only. Jeff Johnstone points out that the J/28, J/34c, J/37c, and J/40 are performance cruisers, and that the J/36, J/35, J/37, and J/44 are cruiser/racers.

The first of the cruisers with racing ability, the J/36, joined the J/Boats fleet in July 1980. This design was inspired by America's Cup helmsman, Bob Bavier (who owned a J/30). Speaking of the new designs, Rod said,

"Big-time sailors and sailmakers loved the J/24, but the J/30 and J/36 were not designed for grand prix racing (IOR), so we took a lot of flack from the pros . . . ."

That negative outlook from some racers did not entirely affect sales of the two boats. Rod continued, "[We] sold a lot of boats until the recession killed sales of the J/36 and J/30 in 1982."

The J/30 was a success as a one-design racer, but sales of the J/36 did not reach the

design's potential. Even so, J/Boats sold a respectable 55 J/36s, and the boat won its class in the Rolex Cup at St. Thomas, U.S. Virgin Islands, in 1981.

As the new designs came off the drawing board with Rod continuing to work out of his Stonington home, Bob found he needed more space for the company's operations. He rented an old six-room colonial house at 24 Mill Street in Newport and moved in. The staff remained small: Bob, a sales manager, and a

J/41s took first through fourth places in the One-Ton North American Championship in 1984 and placed a respectable third and fifth overall in SORC the same year.

". . . A performance cruiser that's fast, simple to sail, and easy to handle;" those were some of the parameters for the J/40, which was completed as a well-appointed 40-footer.

Launched in June 1988, the J/33 is a competitive Performance Handicap Racing Fleet (PHRF) cruiser/racer. It comes equipped with accommodation for weekend cruising, yet can hold its own on the race course. Like so many of her earlier sisters, the J/33 has won major races on both coasts as well as on the Great Lakes.

Opposite page: A J/40 cruises slowly with spinnaker pulling and mainsail set in light airs. When it was launched in 1985, the J/40 set a new standard for fast and safe cruisers.

The J/33 is constructed from Lloyd's approved Baltek Contourkore end-grained balsa laminate using biaxial and unidirectional glass roving, with interplastic vinylester resin on the outer hull layer for optimum blistering resistance.

A cruising version of the J/34, the J/34c makes for an ideal long-distance voyaging and live-aboard boat. One couple sailed the Caribbean for two years in comfort on their J/34c.

secretary. Naturescapes, Bob and Mary's own company, also took space in the house for its sole employee, a sales representative.

Rod referred to J/Boats' reaction to the 1982 recession as having to find the "maximum bang for the buck." In other words, it was all about getting the boat speed up and production costs down.

"The key," he said, "was in TPI's ability for quick start-up in production of new designs."

By then, competitors were closing in on J/Boats' J/24 and J/30 markets with new and fast offshore one-design boats between 30 and 35 feet.

When a new 30-footer, the J/29, first sailed in 1982, it was, in essence, a J/30 sawed off at the top. Designed to be affordable in the recession years of the 1980s, the J/29 sold for considerably less than its near relative.

As Rod put it: "The J/29 was the 'quick-fix' MORC racer. Bob called me on April Fool's

Day and asked me how quick we could come up with a first-to-finish MORC boat that would beat the Olsen 30 at the MORC Internationals in three months. I told him we had already designed and built the cruising version—the J/30. All we needed to do for the racing version was to strip it out (no furniture or diesel), design a slightly deeper keel, lower the deck, cabin, and sheer line, make it lighter, and put more sail on it. We left the rig the same, and we also came out with a masthead rig version, which rated better under the MORC rule."

Two months later, J/Boats launched the "racing" version of the J/30, thanks to the wizardry of Everett Pearson in adapting to the sudden marketing need. It was a racer, and it was hard to beat. J/29s finished first, second, third, and fourth at the Block Island Race Week. Inevitably, there were compromises, or concessions in the design. Whereas the J/30 is equipped as a cruiser with standing head room

Another pocket cruiser, the J/28 is a smaller version of the J/40 with most of the same cruising equipment. Sixty-eight hulls were built, and the design has earned a cult-like status with J boat owners.

Rabbit, a Newport, Rhode Island–based J/28 at anchor, shows its cruising design to great effect.

Opposite page: *Hoodlum* picks up speed under spinnaker. The J/33 is actually faster than most cruiser/racers 3 or 4 feet longer. Spacious and uncluttered decks equate to room to move safely while racing, or to relax while day sailing.

in the cabin, the J/29 is significantly faster without losing any of the J/30's stability. The sailing public, the ultimate arbiters of a boat's success, gave it a definite thumbs up. A fraction less than 300 J/29 hulls took to the water before production ceased in 1987, including several built under license by Nissan's marine division in Japan.

Although some J/30 owners felt that the popularity of their design lessened with the introduction of the J/29, Bob Johnstone disagreed. He pointed out that J/30 sales were revitalized by the new boat, in part because the J/29 attracted prospective owners to dealerships who then ended up choosing the heavier J/30 as a more practical solution to their family needs, despite its higher price tag.

Keeping Boats Affordable

As the J/29 was a development of the J/30, so the J/22—launched in May 1983—was J/Boats' answer to the dealers' requests for an affordable entry-level sailing boat. They wanted a boat

they could sell for under $10,000, which is where the J/24 used to be. A secondary consideration was for a boat that could be sold in fleets to yacht clubs, colleges, and community boating programs, particularly in harbors where J/Boats did not have a dealer presence. Ideal for novice sailors, due to its light weight and ease of handling, the J/22 has become popular with sailing schools as an alternative to the ever-popular J/24. To date, there are in excess of 1,550 J/22s sailing in 65 fleets in 18 countries.

In 2005, the J/22 was chosen for the Rolex International Women's Keelboat Championship in Annapolis, Maryland, the third time it has served in that role. Held every two years since its inception in 1985, the event used J/24s for its first eight championships. The J/22s are built in Italy, South Africa, and the United States. In 1994, 11 years after it appeared, the J/22 would be distinguished as an international class by the International Sailing Federation (ISAF), the world's governing body for sailing. The J/24 was honored with the same distinction in 1981.

The first of the J cruisers with racing ability, the J/36's design was inspired by America's Cup helmsman Bob Bavier, even though it was not designed for grand prix racing.

A stripped-out racing version of the J/30, the J/29 has been competing with honors at racing events since her introduction in the summer of 1982. Here, a J/29 is seen in the Yukon Cup race at the 2000 Key West Race Week.

More than 1,550 J/22s sail in 65 fleets in 18 countries. In 1984, the ISAF granted the J/22 International Class status.

The fin keel J/36 on stands—55 of the design were sold before the recession of the early 1980s effectively halted sales.

The J/35, launched in the spring of 1983, was another answer to the downturn in the U.S. economy. It was a modification of the J/36 with a considerably lower price tag— $30,000 less at $49,500. Other important differences included a masthead rig instead of fractional, an improved keel, and a lower center of gravity, plus a tiller instead of a wheel. The interior showed changes too. Some of the standard cabin fittings on the J/36 became options on the J/35. The boat was an instant success with over 170 hulls sold in the first three years. The J/35 remained in production until 1992, selling 325 in total. J/35 one-design racing remains active in North America.

"Even now, there's hardly a boat out there of its size that can beat a J/35 'round the buoys," said Rod of the boat he calls "a juiced-up, stripped-out J/36." The design was no slouch offshore either. A J/35 was the fastest entrant under 40 feet in the 1984 Newport-to-Bermuda race.

Another cruiser/racer, the J/37, joined the J/Boats roster in the mid 1980s. When it came on the market, it was touted as "the fastest J boat yet." Its hull shape was inspired by the J/35 and its interior by the J/40.

One year after its launch, the J/37 won its class in three major races and justified its billing as the fastest J boat to date.

The American Sailboat Hall of Fame standard reads: "A boat that has earned lasting recognition by fostering new enjoyment and growth in the sport of sailing through excellent design and production ingenuity." The election committee obviously appreciated the J/35's values; it was inducted into the hall of fame to join the J/24.

New Boats, Continued Successes

With the exception of 1981, J/Boats introduced at least one new boat each year throughout the 1980s. Without exception, they all made a significant mark in some form or other. As an example, 1983's J/41s took third and fifth places overall in the 1984 SORC, and first through

Easily recognized as a J boat, the J/37 looks just as ready to cruise far offshore as it does to win races anywhere in the world.

fourth in the One-Ton North American Championship the same year. It also won its division in the Newport-to-Bermuda race, earned the Mumm Merit Award for Design in 1985, and was overall winner in the SORC.

The company's first purpose-built cruising sailboat, the J/40, was the end result of a brand survey conducted by *Sailing World* magazine. The magazine polled its readers to learn (if they were to buy another boat) which brand they would choose and what size boat they would want. According to Bob Johnstone, J/Boats garnered 84 percent of the vote. In typical fashion, Bob's immediate concern was, "Well, who are these other 16 percent, the ones who preferred competing brands?"

Bob asked to see the interview sheets and learned that about half those who responded to the poll hoped or planned to buy a larger luxury cruising boat, somewhere between 38 and 44 feet. Based on the premise that J/Boats' business is a function of people coming into the J family or leaving it and going to a different supplier, Bob said, "We needed to offer them a really nicely equipped cruising boat of

about 40 feet: a performance cruiser that's fast, simple to sail, and easy to handle."

Rod designed the J/40 to meet those requirements. It showed its breeding and proved itself equal to the company's by-then rather illustrious name, by winning its class in the Chicago–Mackinac Race in its first year. *Sailing World* magazine voted the J/40 Overall Boat of the Year. Meanwhile, the J/34 achieved its own recognition as the best-selling IOR design in America.

Two more cruising yachts—the J/28 and J/37—came off the drawing board in 1986. The J/28 was a pocket-cruiser version of the J/40, complete with most of the same cruising amenities. Like the J/40, it would achieve a cult-like status with J owners, rarely appearing on the secondhand market. Even when it did so, it would command nearly full value. The J/37 hit the market as the "fastest J boat yet," with a J/35-inspired hull shape and foils, and a J/40 interior. It raised the dual-purpose cruiser/racer bar another notch and foreshadowed the coming of the J/44. A year after its launch, a J/37—a cruising sailboat, remem-

ber—won its class in three major races. Twenty-four J/35s entered the Block Island Race series off Rhode Island in 1986, making that racer America's fastest-growing big boat one-design.

During the 1980s, J boats continued to take home the silver from racing events on the U.S. East and West coasts, on the Great Lakes, in the Caribbean, and at Cowes Week in the United Kingdom.

Bigger Boats

In May 1989, the company unveiled its biggest boat to date. The J/44 came about following an analysis of the Newport-to-Bermuda race. The company management and design team had asked themselves a pertinent question: "If we decide to build a larger cruising boat other than the existing J/40, how long would it have to be?" After a detailed study of past Bermuda races and the boat sizes and categories entered, the next step was to analyze the qualities of each boat. As a result of the study, the J/Boats team knew its next boat would be

a little over 44 feet but less than 45 feet. Bob explained the reasoning: "There's something intimidating to some buyers about a boat that's 45 feet or more."

Designed to be an optimally sized cruiser/racer—a boat an owner would not be concerned about taking offshore—the J/44 became one of the most successful offshore American yacht designs of its size ever built. As the 1980s came to a close, J/Boats had the pleasure of seeing a J/44 win the New York Yacht Club's Queen's Cup on one side of the Atlantic and win at Cowes Week on the European side of the ocean. To cap all the achievements, *Sailing World* magazine voted the J/44 Overall Boat of the Year, and a J/37c (a new, more cruising-oriented version of the J/37) was the overall Performance Handicap Racing Fleet (PHRF) winner at Block Island Race Week.

Jeff Johnstone stressed: "Each design has its own unique story, its own reason for existence. You could probably write a book about each one, just based on the many unique experiences of the owners."

Light, airy, and functional, the J/44's cabin interior was designed with cruising in mind.

Iona, a J/44, up to speed with a full crew on the windward rail—67 J/44s were built between 1989 and 1993. The design was the first to be given a separate start at the Newport-to-Bermuda race. It has its own active one-design class association.

When the J/44 was unveiled in May 1989, it was the biggest boat the company had produced to date. An optimally sized cruiser/racer for offshore use, the J/44 won the New York Yacht Club's Queen's Cup, as well as Cowes Week in England.

A performance-cruising version of the J/37, a J/37c showed its racing ability by taking overall honors at Block Island Race Week as the 1980s came to a close.

Five

Under New Management

A
ny new business tends to be cyclical, and J/Boats
was no exception. "We went through a series of
cycles when we had to tighten our belts and take
less money out of the company," Bob explained.
"Economic conditions generally forced us to be
creative, to really re-stage the company. That happened several times,
one of which was in 1981 and 1982, when the market bottomed."

The recessions of that era took their toll on boat sales, and J/Boats
suffered along with other builders. "We finally got out of that one by
coming up with new versions of the J/30 and J/36, and introducing the
J/22. In effect, we re-staged our previous launches with lower-priced but
better-performing versions of other designs." The J/29 went on the market
with a selling price of $25,000, about $17,000 cheaper than the J/30. Similarly,
the J/35 was markedly less expensive than the J/36. The ploy proved an
intelligent one. The new models sold well, and the company realized
an increase in sales for the J/30 at the same time.

Opposite page:
Although it was launched
before the younger
generation of Johnstones
took over the J/Boats
helm, the J/40 cruiser
came on the scene
while Alan, Stuart, and
Drake worked for the
company under Rod
and Bob's direction.

J World Sailing School, started by Stuart, Drake, and Jeff Johnstone in 1981, used J/24s to teach adults how to sail in week-long immersion courses, keeping the students out on the water for six or more hours each day.

Between them, Rod and Bob Johnstone have six sons. All accomplished sailors and experienced racers, three of the oldest were about to make their own small but significant mark in the sailing world.

"Stuart and Drake, Bob's oldest two sons, called me in April 1981 and asked me if I would be interested in joining them in a sailing school enterprise," Jeff Johnstone explained. "The fact is, none of us really wanted to go and work for J/Boats. We'd had a lot of fun being involved in it, but to come right out of college and go to work for our fathers was not what we wanted. None of us even contemplated the idea. We'd all been teaching sailing at different clubs for some time; in fact, I was already committed to teaching at a club in Connecticut that summer, and Stu and Drake were well into the planning stage to launch an off-the-beach Sunfish/Hobie Cat school in Newport."

After a businesslike discussion, the three boys agreed to go into business together in a company they would call J World Sailing School. The new company's mission was to teach adults as opposed to kids, employing Sunfish and Hobie Cats as the training vehicles.

Before the boys purchased the required vessels, Rod and Bob, seeing an opportunity for J/Boats, suggested their sons should perhaps teach sailing in J/24s. Jeff, Stuart, and Drake agreed.

The three boys each invested $3,500 in the new company. Jeff raised his share by, as he put it, "creatively shifting around my work load at college." Rod had given Jeff his tuition funds for the fall semester. Jeff put the money to good use.

Rod and Bob helped J World financially by signing the original loan on the boats. "Because no bank wanted to talk to three 21-year-olds just out of college with no assets," Jeff noted. What little money the trio had went into producing brochures. "Rod and Bob, as J/Boats, Inc., basically promised the bank that if we messed up, they would buy the boats back."

J World had a very successful first summer in Newport. "With the mantra of the school being 'learn more in a week,'" Jeff explained, "we gave our students full-immersion courses, having them out on the water for six or seven hours each day. The J/24 became the perfect vehicle. It is so responsive. You pull the back-stay down a bit, you make some sort of small

Masts, sleek hulls, and bright-red J pennants announce the powerful presence of the J boat fleet at the annual Newport, Rhode Island, boat show—home territory for the company.

By the time the younger generation of Johnstones took over the management of the company, the J/35 had garnered strong acceptance from boaters. The design enjoyed a long production life, with 330 built between 1983 and 1992.

The J/Boats presence at the Stamford, Connecticut, boat show in 1985. A fine collection of models are gathered, including J/24, J/41, J/29, J/27, J/35, and J/22.

sail adjustment, and the students could sense the difference immediately. So they learned quicker. This became our lifestyle for a couple of years."

In Jeff's case, the lifestyle lasted for several years. He continued, "We started to set up other schools and developed a nomadic life. We'd start with summers here in Newport, then have the winter in Key West. Then we added San Diego and San Francisco. And that's how we kind of got into the boat business. We had a good first summer and were able to sell the boats through a local dealer before we had to start paying for [winter] storage. Then we

ordered six new boats for the winter program in Key West. For a period of about three or four sessions, we just kept buying and selling the J/24s we needed. I suppose, in retrospect, we became one of the better J/24 dealers. For Rod and Bob it was ideal, probably their plan all along. And that somewhat set the stage for later. Once we'd run the school for a few years, each of us eventually went on to work for J/Boats."

During this time, Jeff's younger brother Phil ran the J World office.

Stuart left the day-to-day management of J World and joined J/Boats full-time as marketing

and regatta/promotions manager in 1984, a position he would hold for six years. During his tenure, in 1985, the company introduced its first purpose-built cruising sailboat, the J/40.

The company structure at the time was still small. A staff of four, including Bob (president) and Stuart (marketing), worked out of the office at 24 Mill Street in Newport, and Rod continued to design from Stonington. Stuart spent much of his time in the field, attending boat shows and sailing with owners and potential owners to promote the boats.

Drake Johnstone, Bob's second son, became sales manager in 1986. He held the position until 1991, when he left the day-to-day operation of the company to pursue a business degree.

A New Team

As often happens with family-run companies, especially when highly competitive siblings are involved, a period of petty conflicts occurred in the mid-1980s. Individually, none of them were serious, but combined they could have proved disruptive. Harmony was finally restored to the family and the company in late 1987 when Bob came up with what he referred to as a "secession strategy" for J/Boats, Inc. In simple terms, that plan entailed getting the next generation involved in running the company. Sons on both sides were skilled sailors, all were knowledgeable about the boating business, and they were all well-educated. The recipe for continued success under a new team was a strong one.

Bob said, "I felt the person running J/Boats should be a natural conciliator. Of all our offspring, I believed [Rod's son] Jeff had the strongest skills along those lines, so we [Bob and Rod] discussed the idea."

The company already employed Bob's sons, Stuart and Drake, plus Rod's youngest son, Alan. Recalling those early years in the company, Alan Johnstone said, "I was really into windsurfing, rather than keelboat sailing back then. After a couple of years of college, I decided to learn the sailmaking trade, and after that I spent some time in yacht charter management. I started working with Rod in 1985. I consider the years 1985 to 1987 to be

The Annapolis Boat Show in Maryland is one of the major boat shows on the East Coast. J/Boats always has a strong showing and attracts attention to its on-the-water displays.

Launched in 1991, the J/105 has grown into large fleets across the United States and beyond. Here, a fleet with spinnakers flying makes the downwind run on San Francisco Bay.

my apprenticeship years, when I worked in Rod's home design office in Stonington. During those years, I enrolled in the same [boat] design correspondence course that Rod had taken years before, and developed a love for boat design."

Rod wanted Alan to be part of the new management equation as well, and for Phil—by then a lawyer—to take on legal responsibilities. Bob proposed that he and Rod bow out of the company as far as holding office and being members of the board were concerned. They

would, of course, continue as joint stockholders. In addition, Rod would continue in his role as chief designer and Bob would continue his role as product strategist and marketer.

When the restructuring took place in December 1987, Jeff Johnstone emerged as president, and Alan, Stuart, and Drake as vice presidents, with Stuart becoming chairman of the board. Bob no longer worked out of the company's offices to avoid the possibility of the new and younger team deferring to him on important decisions. He and Rod wanted them

The J/37c cruiser was featured at an indoor display at the New York Boat Show when it was launched in 1989.

"Round-the-buoys" racing at its best—a well-heeled J/105 gets its lee rail wet while showing its form during a race on San Francisco Bay.

When the J/160 was launched at the end of 1995, it was the largest J boat to that date. At 53 feet LOA, the magnificent cruising yacht would not be surpassed in size by another J boat for close to a decade.

to become good at their new jobs, to become good managers in their own right.

"The only way that could work out," Bob said, "was to let them suffer a little, to work through their own problems and come to us only if they needed our expertise in the final analysis."

Another concern was that, if Bob and Rod constantly hung around the office, the younger management team might not stick with the job—they might move on to alternative endeavors.

Without the company's two original members, the board of directors became Jeff, Phil, Alan, Stuart, and Drake. Phil took his seat on the board of directors after he graduated from the University of Pennsylvania with a degree in law. He had no interest in being an employee, yet he wanted to be involved. "It was important for me to be a part of the company, but at arm's length," he said. In addition to serving on the board, Phil is company secretary and attorney.

When the founding principals of J World Sailing School moved on, the school, with six locations nationwide, continued to function under new management. It is now in its 25th

Jim Johnstone, son of Rod and Bob's younger brother, John, is the J/Boats sales manager based at the company offices in Newport, Rhode Island. Jim led his crew to a third-place finish in the J/105 one-design series at the 2005 Key West Race Week.

Jeff Johnstone, Rod Johnstone's eldest son, was a sailing instructor and partner in J World Sailing School before he became president of J/Boats, Inc. in 1988. He continues to race J boats whenever he can get away from work.

Alan Johnstone is Rod Johnstone's youngest son. A vice president of J/Boats, Inc., he is a yacht designer like his father and works with him on most models. Alan designed the J/32 and the J/109.

Rod Johnstone designed the J/92 for family participation. She has great stability and highly efficient systems, which make it easier to sail with a couple of people, instead of a team of specialists.

There are currently 17 fleets coast to coast in the USA J/80 International Class Association. Overseas, it was reported that the French navy ordered 50 J/00s for use as training boats.

A fleet of J/80s, the family "rocket ship," driving downwind under spinnakers. There are now J/80 International Class Associations in France, Germany, Sweden, the United Kingdom, and the United States.

year of operation and is still a good customer for J/Boats.

Discussing his part in the new regime, Alan Johnstone said, "My position here at J/Boats is to spearhead the effort for new projects, and I've played an increasingly important design role in each model since 1988. For most J/Boat models, Rod is the designer of record. The two complete J models that I take credit for are the J/32 and the J/109. Rod and

I have a healthy back-and-forth communication on all new models. While trying times exist in all father-son relationships, overall, it is a pleasure for me to [have] worked with my father for twenty years now."

The new management took over in the heyday of real estate market booms. Although they made no radical changes in the company's operations, Jeff acknowledges that the new management team did make

several adjustments. "We had the immediate advantage of more human resources. This allowed us to cover more ground and ultimately better serve the owners and dealers. At any given time we could have six people spread around the globe giving clinics, sailing with owners, or attending boat shows."

Through Bob's efforts J/Boats already had a few dealers in Italy, Holland, and the United Kingdom, but the company did not have a consistent presence at European boat shows and related events. At that time, in the fall of 1990, exchange rates were favorable for U.S. exports, and the U.K. market in particular seemed ready for the bigger Js.

Rod said, "We all agreed in 1990 that we needed a J/Boats presence throughout Europe—in the form of active sales and distribution of our boats, as well as a loyal dealer basis. We did have a large following in the J/24 and J/22 classes, but our larger designs were basically unknown. We felt that we had designs to offer that would be potentially popular in Europe in addition to the J/24. Stuart was ready, willing, and able to move to the U.K. for a few years with his wife, Shelley, to get the ball rolling."

Jeff added, "Most of the top racing boats in the U.K. at the time were fractional rigged, so when Stu brought in both the J/35 and J/44

The J/Boats team in the summer of 1995. Resting on the boom of a J/42 are (left to right) Jim, Bob, Rod, Jeff, and Alan.

A pair of racing J/120s with colorful spinnakers flying runs downwind past a moored cruise ship and the masts of a tall ship in the Caribbean.

Opposite page: Over 210 J/120s have been built. They sail on waters as far apart as Sweden and Australia, Taiwan and South Africa, and from Japan to Chile, with the largest numbers in the United States.

(both masthead-rigged boats), and began winning races, it turned a lot of heads."

In 1992: J/Boats Europe was formed as a distributorship, with Stuart coordinating European dealer activities from his base in England. Jeff Johnstone explained, "Within two years a dealer network was well established, and the larger Js were on the map, winning events in the U.K., France, Netherlands, Sweden, and Germany. As the U.S. dollar began to regain strength, it became apparent that a European builder of larger Js would be needed to supply the network. Stuart led the charge and was instrumental in signing up the French builder (J Composite) in 1994. J Composite later became J Europe, which currently builds six J models between 26 feet and 43 feet."

In 1995, with the European operation in good shape, the parent company in the United States took over the J/Boats Europe reins, and Stuart and Shelley moved home to America. At that juncture, Stuart left the company but retained his position on the board.

The J/Boats' core—Rod, Bob, Jeff, Alan, and latterly Jim (John Johnstone's son) as sales manager—brainstorm ideas based on possible boats one of them would like to own and that Bob knows he could market effectively. They then hand the idea over to Rod and Alan who, between them, work out what can be done and what cannot be done.

"We're really the practical arm of the company," said Alan. "We take the collective marketing concept and come up with the best possible combination of elements, within chosen constraints, to make a great sailboat. Rod has his own convictions about the sailboat he wants and there's often a

healthy tension that develops between he and I, and the group as a whole, during the creative process. Rod is incredibly talented as a sailboat designer. I have tons of respect for him for that reason. But I have my own ideas and convictions too. Ultimately, Rod draws most of the final hull designs, and I handle details and drawings of other components in the design. Included are creating deck, rig, and interior arrangement drawings; weight studies; keel and rudder designs, as well as 3D models for new projects. Rod and I constantly go back and forth a lot on a large number of design subjects on a daily basis."

Speaking of the company as a family unit, Alan added: "We all love to sail, and sharing this joy with our families is the number one priority. Ultimately, our passion for the sport and our families is what drives us to create new and better sailboats. It's a privilege to be able to earn a living doing something we love to do."

A New Learning Curve

The racing honors continued to accumulate under the new leadership, as did the introduction of new models. National economics, however, were about to create a certain amount of stress for the new team.

"We [the new management] had to deal with the luxury tax/recession in 1990–1991.

That was probably the biggest lesson learned: how to stay focused on what you do best," said Jeff Johnstone.

The implementation of the U.S. government's ill-considered luxury excise tax on January 1, 1990, caused many a hiccup in the leisure boating industry. Boats weren't the only items targeted. Automobile and private aircraft builders suffered too. The tax applied to the "first retail sale" of luxury goods with a retail sales price above $100,000, in the case of pleasure boats. The new tax certainly made life difficult for the young Johnstones, as it did for so many others, but they kept their heads. For potential buyers of boats in the targeted bracket, J/Boats, TPI Composites, and their dealers nationwide kicked in one-third of the new tax to keep sales moving. Those opposed to the tax—and they were many—could see that the effect would not just hit consumers in their wallets. A ripple effect would, inevitably, spread throughout the industries affected and culminate in lost jobs; and it did. As a direct result of the luxury tax, boat builders in Florida had to lay off 5,000 laborers at the end of 1990.

Despite the problems associated with the new tax, the company's profile continued to shine. In 1991, *Fortune* magazine honored J/Boats, Inc. by naming the company's performance sailboats one of the 100 best products manufactured in America.

J/32 hull number 1, *Whistler*, on a test sail on Narragansett Bay, Rhode Island. Designed to sail well under mainsail alone and cruise with a small jib rather than a genoa. Alan Johnstone's design was built to cruise, but also performs well as a racer.

Opposite page: J/160s have crossed the major oceans while cruising as far north as Iceland and Scandinavia, and as far south as Cape Horn. They have survived a tsunami and the angry seas of the Agulhas Current off the South African coast.

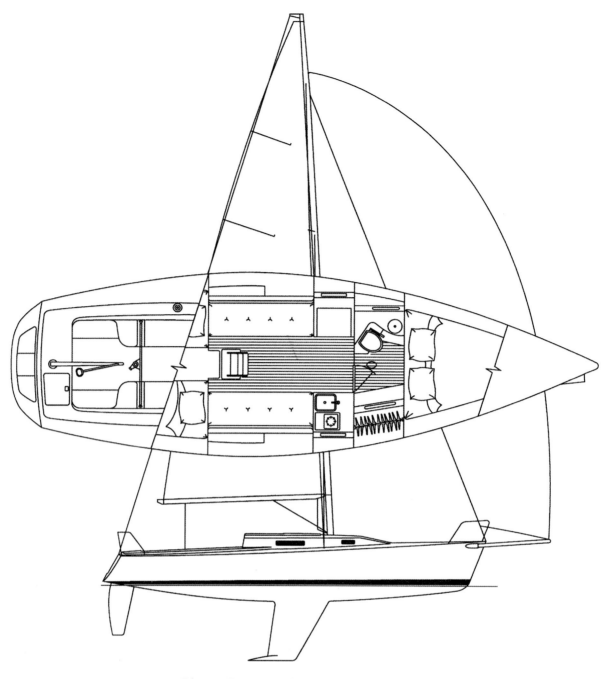

J/105 Principal Dimensions

LOA	34.5 feet	10.51 meters	I	40.6 feet	12.37 meters
LWL	29.5 feet	8.99 meters	ISP	42.1 feet	12.83 meters
Beam	11.0 feet	3.35 meters	J	13.5 feet	4.12 meters
Draft	6.5 feet	1.98 meters	P	41.5 feet	12.65 meters
Displacement	7,750 pounds	3,515 kilograms	E	14.6 feet	4.45 meters
Engine	18 horsepower	18 horsepower	SA/Dspl	24	24
Lead keel	3,400 pounds	1,542 kilograms	Dspl/L	135	135
100% SA	577 square feet	53.6 square meters			

Rod and Bob Johnstone may have stepped aside from the day-to-day running of the company, but they continue to be heavily involved, each in his own field. Rod is still the driving force behind most of the designs, and Bob, the marketing guru, writes much of the advertising copy. Bob also has his own boat ideas, plus a say in each of the new ideas proposed by his brother, his sons, and his nephews. Always keen to be out sailing, Rod and Bob rarely miss the launch of a new model. When asked who takes each new design out for its sea trials, Rod's face stretched into that alligator grin and he replied, "I do." And Bob usually goes too.

Alan Johnstone designed the J/32 cruiser and saw it launched in August 1996. On its sea trials, it proved fast and easy to sail. Delivering hull number 1, *Whistler*, from Rhode Island to Mamaroneck, New York, skipper Robbie Robinson wrote, "[It] encouraged thoughts like, 'If I can fly like this, maybe I can walk on water too.'"

Designer Alan Johnstone and his wife, Laurie, take J/32, *Whistler*, for a test sail.

Six

Cruising, Near and Far

While the racers of the many J boat fleets continued to win at coastal and lake events worldwide, in addition to a number of ocean circuits, a small group of hardy individuals and their crews looked beyond the buoys. Some chose to cruise along the East and West coasts of America, close to land. Others turned their sights considerably farther offshore.

Only four or five decades ago, one could count on the fingers of one hand the number of small boats known to be sailing across vast oceans. Often, they made headline news. But by the 1990s, that had all changed. More and more sailing couples, and single handers, were setting off to explore beyond the horizon. Following in the wake of such luminaries as the great Joshua Slocum, Harry Pigeon, and Bernard Moitessier, a veritable fleet of adventurers set sail to see the world. Not surprisingly, once J/Boats, Inc. developed its line of cruising boats, a succession of well-equipped Js also turned elegant sterns to the land and set sail to cross the seven seas.

Opposite page:
The magnificent J/160. At 53 feet LOA, she is big and strong and ideally suited to long-distance cruising. J/160s have circumnavigated the globe, sailing far to the north and the south, as well as on warm tropical waters.

The J/42's low center of gravity gives her greater stability and improved sail-carrying ability. Combined, they add up to a sea-kindly vessel that one person can handle safely.

The first dedicated cruiser from J/Boats, the J/40, appeared in June 1985. Designed, as usual, by Rod Johnstone, the boat proved an unqualified success—so much so that the first dedicated cruiser of the 1990s, the J/42, launched in June 1995, was based on the original J/40 hull shape. The J/42 was followed by the magnificent 53-foot J/160 at the end of the year.

The first J boat designed exclusively by Alan Johnstone, another cruiser, arrived in August 1996. Twenty-one feet shorter than the J/160, Alan's J/32 filled a definite void in the marketplace, and a bevy of knowledgeable sailors took advantage of his new design to sail far offshore.

In the less than 20 years since the first J cruiser arrived on the scene, the various models have made some classic voyages, some long distance, some close to home. One, a J/160 named *Pipe Dream IX*, owned by Dr. Scott Piper of Florida, just keeps going around and around the world.

Long-Distance Cruising

Dr. Piper and an earlier boat, a J/40 known as *Pipe Dream VI*, sailed many thousands of offshore miles between 1988 and 1996, almost certainly making *Pipe Dream VI* the most-traveled J/40 in the world. Initially, Dr. Piper bought the J/40 specifically to race. First, she won the Miami–Montego Bay Race; then, in 1993, she won the Daytona, Florida, to Bermuda race and followed that by taking the Rolex Cup in St. Thomas, U.S. Virgin Islands.

"It was on these long-distance races that I got hooked on cruising," Piper said. "I took several weeks to cruise the boat home after the race and discovered a whole new world."

He later sailed *Pipe Dream VI* to South America, throughout the Caribbean and Central America. After winning the Daytona–Bermuda race in 1993, *Pipe Dream VI* crossed the North Atlantic with a delivery crew, taking 18 days for the passage to the tiny port of Carloway, in the west Hebrides of Scotland. She continued

A J/160, *Flanders*, under spinnaker on Narragansett Bay, Rhode Island. J/Boats advised, "The design mandate for the J/160 was to exceed all prior standards for a cruising yacht of this size."

The Virgin Islands are a popular cruising ground, especially for U.S. East Coast sailors. Leverick Bay, on Virgin Gorda in the British Virgin Islands, is a prime anchorage.

Cape fur seals feed in the rich waters of the Benguela Current, which runs along the South Atlantic coast of Namibia. The seals inhabit large colonies, most notably at Cape Cross, to the north of the old German town of Swakopmund. The J/160 *Pipe Dream IX* called at Namibia in March 2005.

through the dangerous millrace known as the Pentland Firth, between the northern Scottish mainland and the Orkney Islands, to Wick, on Scotland's east coast. From there *Pipedream VI* crossed the North Sea to Kristiansand, Norway, and on to Copenhagen. After a few weeks of cruising in the Baltic, *Pipe Dream VI* turned her bow to the west.

En route home, Piper stopped off in the Canary Islands for a few months. "There, I saw the Round the World Rally pass through and knew what was next," he said. Dr. Piper sold the J/40 and replaced her with a larger boat, the new J/160, in April 1996. That cruiser, *Pipe Dream IX*, joined the Round the World Rally of 1997–1998.

Speaking proudly of his boats, Piper said, "The Js have taken me as far north as Finland and as far south as Cape Horn."

Right: Namibia's great sand dunes spread far along the coast and deep into the interior. As the sun arcs across the sky, the dunes change color, the deepest hues being at sunset and sunrise. The crew of *Pipe Dream IX* saw these dunes during their visit to Namibia.

Opposite page: The old British telephone kiosk on the end of the refueling pontoon is an easily recognized landmark for cruisers visiting Virgin Gorda, British Virgin Islands.

The J/40 at a mooring.
Owners rate the J/40 as
"a performance cruiser
that's fast, simple to sail,
and easy to handle. . . ."
Introduced in 1985, the
design combines
shorthanded sailing
ability with comfort
and speed.

The well-crafted wooden
fittings in the dinette
area of the J/40's cabin
offer comfort, elegance,
and a warm feeling.

Tom Babbitt at the helm of his J/40, *Bravo*. Tom and Jane Babbitt, with their two daughters, sailed 8,000 miles on a year-long cruise from Maine to the Caribbean. *J/Boats, Inc.*

In 2005 *Pipe Dream IX* was on her third circumnavigation under Dr. Piper's command. He has a captain aboard, who takes care of maintenance and looks after the boat in port while Piper flies home for short periods. Once back on board, however, Scott Piper, owner and captain, takes over again. Earlier in 2005, *Pipe Dream IX* was in Cape Town, South Africa, being prepared for the homeward leg of her third circumnavigation. During this voyage, *Pipe Dream IX* passed her 100,000-nautical-mile mark, and sailed to her 92nd country when she visited Namibia, in southwest Africa, soon after departure from Cape Town. Following calls at the South Atlantic islands of St. Helena and Ascension, *Pipe Dream IX*'s course called for a visit to Natal, Brazil, before returning to the United States in mid-March 2005 to complete the circumnavigation. Not one to waste precious adventure-sailing time, Dr. Piper planned to

leave on his fourth circumnavigation in mid-April 2005. Each circumnavigation to date has followed a different course. The same will be true of his fourth round-the-world voyage.

Cruising with Kids

In the J/24's first year of production, John Johnstone and his family cruised regularly along the New England coast in their boat, not always without a certain amount of drama. Sailing between Newport and Marion Harbor in light fog, John called his son, Jimmy, to come to the cockpit. There was no answer. He called again louder, concerned his seven-year-old son might have fallen overboard. Refusing to believe the possibility, he frantically searched the boat and finally found Jimmy fast asleep under some lifejackets in a tiny alcove forward of the V-berth: in the anchor chain

The J/40's navigation station reflects the designers' attention to detail for an offshore cruiser. Varnished wood cabinets and panels add warmth, and the station leaves little to be desired from a cruising point of view.

locker, which makes a favorable comment on the J/24's comfort potential, at least for youngsters.

Dedicated J boat owners Tom and Jane Babbitt of Maine bought a new J/30 in the fall of 1980. They raced and cruised in her for a few summers, including taking baby Laura to sea at the tender age of three weeks, with her three-year-old sister, Mary. With the two kids getting bigger, the Babbitts traded up to a J/35, a boat fully equipped for the cruising lifestyle. "I raced her a bit," Tom admitted, "but preferred cruising because we had a growing family."

Two years later, and by then considering themselves full-time cruisers, Tom and Jane progressed to a J/37, *Bravo*, which they, "raced once—and won, of course." They only kept the J/37 for one season of coastal cruising as they were planning a big adventure. They sold the J/37 and bought a J/40 to go offshore cruising. Between June 1988 and June 1989, they and their two young daughters sailed 8,000 miles in the J/40. On the voyage south to the Caribbean, the Babbitts put their boat on display at the Newport, Rhode Island, and Annapolis, Maryland, boat shows as a fine example of a live-aboard boat.

"She was fully outfitted for everybody's dream cruise," Tom explained. "We'd get the girls up early, about 6:00 a.m., have breakfast, tidy the boat, and get the family ashore so the public could look over the boat during the day. At night we'd move back aboard again."

That cruise lasted for exactly one year and 18 hours, from Maine to Grenada and back again. Home-schooling the two girls—ages 7 and 10 at the time—as they went, the family sailed down the east coast to Florida, across to the Bahamas, offshore to the Virgin Islands, and on to Grenada. Taking their time, the family island hopped from Grenada back to the Virgin Islands.

"J/Boats have great resale value," Tom said. "It's never taken us more than six weeks to sell one of ours."

He cites an excellent example: Coming home from Grenada, Tom advertised the boat for sale in St. Thomas, U.S. Virgin Islands. By the time they reached Norfolk, Virginia, he had sold it by radio to a Maine resident. The Babbitts sailed home, unloaded the boat, tidied her up, and delivered her immediately. Then they loaded the boating gear in the family car

Tom and Jane Babbitt sailed their J/40 from Maine to Grenada and back. They sold the boat by radio on the voyage home and bought another J boat soon after.

J/40s, such as this one at a mooring, have cruised extensively. Scott Piper's *Pipe Dream VI* visited Europe, South America, the Caribbean, and Central America. Others have crossed the Pacific and circumnavigated the globe.

and drove to Annapolis, where they bought a J/34c.

"We lived on that boat in Camden, Maine, for two summers, only moving ashore as winter arrived and the ramp became too slippery for the girls to negotiate to meet the school bus," Tom said. Jane added a reminder that, in many ways, it was easier to live aboard in Camden than it was in the Caribbean because they had modern amenities close by, such as a telephone hookup on the boat and hot showers available on the dock.

When Tom sold the J/34c in 1992 after owning her for three years, the family spent one summer without a boat, their first dry spell for a long time. "I nearly went nuts," Tom said, and Jane concurred. "It was awful without a boat." To get back on the water, they bought a used J/22—at 22.5 feet, the smallest the family had owned for a long time. By this time, the girls were in their teens and spent most of their time ashore. Tom and Jane raced the J/22 occasionally. Mostly they went on what Tom

refers to as "B & B cruises." After sleeping on board for a night and finding conditions a little cramped, they cruised from one coastal port to another during the day and stayed in bed and breakfast houses overnight. It is an interesting variation on the cruising theme.

When the J/22 became too small for comfort as a cruising vessel, the Babbitts moved up to a J/35 again for a few years. In 1998, while recovering from surgery, Tom found a used J/34c advertised in a sailing magazine. On his first day out of the house, he went to see the boat and bought her, all in the space of two hours. "We had her for four years," Tom said. "We upgraded her and cruised extensively . . . raced three times and always made the podium." Jane, who had been sailing since she was five years old, admits that she could still be nervous out on the water. "That second 34c made me an independent sailor," she said.

In April 2003, they graduated to a J/42. Explaining his continued association with the

As the sun sets, a fleet of boats waits at their moorings at the Panama Canal Yacht Club, Cristobal, for permission to transit the Panama Canal from the Caribbean to the Pacific.

When experienced J boat owners Tom and Jane Babbitt bought a used J/22, the smallest boat they had owned for many years, they used it for "bed & breakfast" cruises along the New England coast.

Sailboats transiting the Panama Canal are rafted together and held in the center of each lock by skilled Panamanian line-handlers as the water level rises or falls, depending on the direction of travel.

Large mechanical mules take the place of human line-handlers to guide big ships into and out of the locks on the Panama Canal.

J/Boats designs, Tom said, "For us, a J boat makes the whole cruising experience so unthreatening and comfortable." He went further to say, "These boats are so agile, we sail off and back on to our moorings 90 percent of the time. A lost weekend for us is when we have to turn the motor on."

Jane Babbitt summed up her many years of experience with a variety of Js: "They are so easy to sail and I feel safe in them. They have a good righting moment. They are well designed and comfortable to live in. And, we get wherever we're going sooner because they are so fast." Of the J/42, which she rates as her overall favorite, she said: "It's the most luxurious. It's faster and more comfortable [than their previous boats]." Jane does admit that the J/40 has a special place in her heart because of the year the family spent cruising the Caribbean in her.

Voyaging to Paradise

Jeff and Raine Williams, of Rhode Island, sailed their J/40, *Gryphon*, on a six-year circumnavigation between November 1998 and 2004. En route, they cruised the Caribbean, transited the Panama Canal, and explored the Galapagos Islands and a multitude of South Pacific paradises, including the Marquesas, Tahiti, Moorea, Bora Bora, and the Cook Islands before reaching New Zealand. After a flying break back to the United States, their odyssey continued with another cruise through the South Pacific, this time concentrating on islands in the western sector, such as New Caledonia, Niue, and Vanuatu en route to Australia. They followed up with a long crossing of the Indian Ocean to the Malagasy Republic and on to South Africa. The final leg carried

The many beautiful islands of French Polynesia act as magnets for transpacific sailors. Sunsets, such as this one seen from a beach on Moorea, are invariably spectacular events.

The large lagoon at Bora Bora, in French Polynesia, is arguably one of the most idyllic anchorages in the Pacific Ocean. A wide coral reef protects the lagoon from the ocean swell.

Long-range cruising requires careful planning when it comes to diet. Markets like this one in Nadi, Fiji, and other South Pacific islands offer abundant vegetables and fruits.

them up the South Atlantic, with a stop at Ascension Island, to cross the equator and return to the U.S. East Coast.

Since the early days of long-ranging cruising under sail, the South Pacific Islands have ranked high on the list of potential destinations for many offshore sailors. The images of South Seas paradises are well known: coral-ringed lagoons backed by extensive—and usually empty—white or golden sands shaded by palm trees and dominated by verdant mountains. Add predictable sunshine and an abundance of tropical fruits, not forgetting the friendly indigenous peoples, and it is easy to see why so many voyagers turn their bows toward French Polynesia and the multitude of exotic islands scattered across the Pacific Ocean south of the equator.

En route 'round the world, the Williamses found time in paradise to enter *Gryphon* in the third and final week of the 1999 Tonga Cup races. Held off Vava'u and sponsored by the Port Refuge Yacht Club in Neiafu, the Friday afternoon races are open to all comers regardless of size. *Gryphon* won her race. That win was all the more satisfying for the Williamses because a J boat had won each of the previous two Friday events. Charles and Debbie Guildner and family aboard their J/120, *Attitude*, won first. The following week, John and Nancy Moore sailed their J/130, with the delightful name *Break 'N' Wind*, to lead the fleet home. All three winners were cruising yachts, as opposed to racers. As such, they were well stocked with provisions for long-range voyages and, consequently, considerably heavier than

Exotic ports of call heighten the adventure of ocean cruising. The sheltered anchorage at Port Vila, in Vanuatu, is situated between the town and the neighboring island of Irririki.

One of the delights of cruising in the South Pacific is the cultural differences. At Yakel, a traditional village in the forest on Vanuatu's Tanna Island, men, women, and children dance under the shade of a giant banyan tree.

Opposite page:
Launched in 1989, the J/44 has become the most successful large, offshore American yacht design ever, with a total of 67 boats built. With satisfied owners in 14 countries, the design has a long record of ocean passages, regatta wins, and cruising adventures to its credit.

the almost-empty local boats just out for an afternoon's fun on the water.

Echo, a J/160 owned and cruised by John and Nancy Eills, departed Newport, Rhode Island, in 1998 for a west-about circumnavigation. John said, "We took the 'coconut milk run' following South Pacific trade winds." In other words, they transited the Panama Canal, stopped off to explore the Galapagos Islands, then headed straight for the Marquesas and the islands south of the equator. John's plans called for them to be in New Zealand during the America's Cup races for an extended stay. As with many circumnavigators, John and Nancy left their boat in New Zealand and flew home for a few months in the middle of the voyage. For *Echo's* subsequent cruise, scheduled for the summer of 2005, the Eillses planned to explore a few northern ports while circumnavigating Newfoundland. John and Nancy, no strangers to the cooler waters and potentially foggy climes of Canada's maritime provinces, had already explored parts of Nova Scotia and Newfoundland's south shore on a previous cruise.

Sailing North

Ben Blake commissioned his J/160, *Atlantic*, hull number 19, in July 1999. Thanks to the prompting of his eldest son, Adam, Ben planned a transatlantic voyage to Scandinavia for the summer of 2000. At the tender age of seven, Ben and his sister had spent 10 weeks cruising Scandinavian waters with their parents. On that occasion, the parents had shipped the boat to Sweden. A few decades later, Ben wanted to show his own sons the beauties of the Baltic. Adam took the responsibility of suggesting they sail their own boat across the ocean rather than sending it by ship. After some discussion, Ben agreed.

He and his crew—Adam, Cooper, and Morgan (his three sons, ages 22, 20, and 18, respectively)—left Stonington, Connecticut, in the early summer of 2000 with the course set for Reykjavik, Iceland. Ben said, with a certain amount of pride, "We covered 3,000 miles in 14 days at an average speed of just under 9 knots, with almost no motoring."

During one night, the three boys took turns trying to break each other's speed records.

New Zealanders are keen sailors and ever ready to welcome circumnavigators to Auckland's Waitemata Harbour, which is always busy with sailboats, passenger ferries, cargo ships, and cruise liners.

Atlantic had established a personal record of 19.2 knots before the crossing. En route to Iceland, the boys came close by clocking an impressive 18.6 knots. It was exhilarating, but not all plain sailing. In the darkness of a calm night, while probably scudding along about 12 knots with 18-year-old Morgan at the helm, *Atlantic* struck something. Neither Ben nor his crew had any idea what they had hit; only that it had to have been something hard. They speculated on the possibility of a whale or floating debris. As soon as they tied up in Reykjavik, they checked the bow to find it in perfect shape, and they took a look at the keel bolts. There was no visible damage, yet Ben and the boys knew they had hit something solid. When Ben had the boat hauled out in Sweden a couple of months later, he discovered a flattened spot at the bottom of the leading edge of the keel. He surmised that *Atlantic* had tripped over a submerged container, or similar floating obstruction.

After three days sightseeing by car, the Blakes left Iceland to continue east. Two days and one night at sea brought them in sight of the rugged rocks of the Faeroe

Islands, which they visited for two days. Keeping to their northerly track, they called at the Shetland Islands, well north of the Scottish mainland, and on to a Scandinavian landfall at Kristiansand, Norway. By the end of the summer, *Atlantic* had visited a number of Norwegian and Swedish ports, taken a detour to Copenhagen in Denmark, and finished up near Stockholm, where she was hauled out. And there she stayed until the summer of 2002.

Following the long hiatus, Ben and crew flew back to Sweden. They took part in the Gotland Runt, a classic yacht race in Swedish waters, in which they finished poorly. Ben explained: "The Gotland Runt broke our hearts. We were doing very nicely for the first 175-mile slog upwind in heavy air, certainly toward the front of the fleet. Unfortunately, shortly after we turned downwind for what promised to be a spectacular second half, we tore out our only chute and had to limp home unceremoniously, finishing well back on corrected time. We were honored, however, to receive the trophy for having traveled the longest distance to attend the race."

The USS *Peary* memorial at Darwin, in Australia's Northern Territory Scott Piper's J/160 *Pipe Dream IX* called in at Darwin on one of her three circumnavigations to date.

Inland from Darwin, less than a day's drive from the sea, aboriginal art decorates rocks and cliffs in Australia's Outback. This craggy open-air studio is at Manyallaluk, south of Arnhem Land.

Thereafter, *Atlantic* sailed from Stockholm to Germany, where they transited the Kiel Canal to reach Helgoland. Ben had planned to take a look at the Friesien Islands for a few days, but the weather was so good they kept on sailing directly to Amsterdam. *Atlantic* made a few more local stops on the Dutch coast, then crossed the English Channel to make her British landfall at Dover. From there, she followed the south coast of England to Cork in southern Ireland. Just along the coast, Kinsale became the jumping-off point for the homeward crossing.

With time running out, Ben had hoped to sail directly to Nantucket, but a tropical storm convinced him to change course to Halifax, Nova Scotia. On the 15-day voyage from Kinsale, during which they sailed and motored, they actually enjoyed three days of spinnaker runs. As Adam had to be back at work in Boston on a particular date, Ben used the motor more than he had hoped. There was some doubt that Adam would be able to meet his deadline. In fact, keeping in touch with his workmates by e-mail, they were able to run a

lottery on his arrival time. When *Atlantic* pulled into Halifax, on a Sunday, the fuel tank held no more than 3 1/2 gallons of diesel. Adam caught the last flight out that night and reported for work on Monday morning as planned.

The Blakes are not the only J boat owners to enjoy northern climes. Ned Cabot and his crew took *Cielita*, a brand-new J/46, to Greenland in 2003. Built with an additional 1,000 pounds of fiberglass in her hull for reinforcement, particularly in the forward section, *Cielita* was ready for the ice of the Labrador Sea and Davis Strait when she left the factory. Cabot sailed out of Portsmouth, Rhode Island, for Nova Scotia's Cape Breton Island and the lovely Bras d'Or Lakes for a shakedown cruise. Once he was satisfied with his charge, Cabot headed north through the Gulf of St. Lawrence to the Straits of Belle Isle, between the island of Newfoundland and Labrador on the mainland. Safely through the straits and cruising north, *Cielita* called in at Cartwright, Labrador—her final stop before Greenland. On the eight-week cruise, covering 5,000 miles, *Cielita* made her way without mishap through

A J/160, similar to Scott Piper's Pipe Dream IX, which has circumnavigated the world three times, calling at a series of exotic ports.

Opposite page:
Anchoring within swimming distance of pristine beaches and shady palms draws cruisers to the Caribbean and the South Pacific.

The J/42L is a live-aboard version of the J/42 cruiser, which was based on the original J/40 hull shape.

Ned Cabot, center, tells J/160 owners Ben Blake (left) and John Eills (right) about his voyage to western Greenland in his J/46, *Cielita*, in the summer of 2003.

fields of broken and scattered ice as far north as Disko Island, which she circumnavigated, and then wandered down the rugged west coast of Greenland as far as Nuuk. From Nuuk, she again crossed the Davis Strait to Saglek Bay in northern Labrador before following the coast south toward somewhat warmer seas and home.

Many other Js cruise the world. Among them are Peter and Carol Willhauer, who have lived aboard their red J/42-L, *Eight Bells*, for five years. And they don't mind racing occasionally. They entered a West Marine

Carib 1500 rally from Hampton, Virginia, to Tortola, British Virgin Islands, finishing first in their class and second overall out of a fleet of 52 boats.

Bill and Judy Stellin sailed and raced their J/42, *Jaywalker*, getting to know her intimately on the Great Lakes for four years before venturing on to the briny. Confident of their own ability and with complete faith in their boat, they crossed the Atlantic from Rhode Island to Portugal in 2000. Since then, they have cruised extensively throughout the Mediterranean.

Ned Cabot's J/46, *Cielita*, passes a huge iceberg in the Davis Strait off the west coast of Greenland. *Cielita* spent two months cruising in the icy northern waters in the summer of 2003.

Cielita, under spinnaker alone, cruises sedately past the foot of a glacier coursing through rugged terrain on Greenland's west coast. The specially strengthened J/46 acquitted herself well on the northern voyage, whether in heavy seas or working through scattered pack ice. *Cielita*'s next major voyage is across the Atlantic via Greenland's east coast and Iceland.

In Harm's Way

Inevitably, on long-distance voyages, some cruisers inadvertently position themselves in the path of impending danger without any way of knowing it. When the deadly tsunami smashed into Southeast Asia's coastline on December 26, 2004, at least two J boats, as well as many other makes, stood in the way. Part of the Blue Water Cruising Rally, an organized circumnavigation, *Condor*, a J/160 owned by a Britains David and Claire Lewis, and *Aragorn*, a J/46 owned by Richard and Catherine York, had reached Phuket, Thailand, in mid-December 2004. Over Christmas, *Condor* stayed in Phuket while *Aragorn* rested at anchor off Phi Phi Don, a small island to the east of Phuket.

In the early morning of December 26, an earthquake measuring 8.9 on the Richter scale shook the seabed off the northwest coast of Sumatra, a little over 300 statute miles from Phuket. As a direct result of the disturbance, a tsunami, or tidal wave, radiated out from the

epicenter of the earthquake at deadly speed. A series of tidal waves, following each other in quick succession, raced toward land. In a bay at Phi Phi Don, a popular tourist destination, the tide was high. The first indication boaters had of the fast-approaching danger came when the bay rapidly drained of water in a counter-clockwise whirlpool effect. Boats dragged their anchors, some bounced on the bottom. Those with crews on board got out of the bay as fast as possible. At least three large angry waves roared into the bay that morning, creating unimagined death and destruction on land. Exercising instinctive seamanship, Richard York and his crew got *Aragorn* to safety. Both *Aragorn* and *Condor* survived the tsunami intact, as did their fortunate crews.

Condor's planned two-year voyage started in Newport, Rhode Island, in December 2002. She spent most of 2003 island hopping through the Caribbean before joining the long-distance rally and transiting the Panama Canal in February 2004. *Aragorn* had left New York in October 2003.

According to J/Boats, the J/46 is a "maxi-Ditch" yacht, the tallest yacht that can fit under the bridges of the Intracoastal Waterway. Ned Cabot's *Cielita*, which he sailed to Greenland, is a J/46.

The J/33, launched in 1988, is a competitive Performance Handicap Racing Fleet (PHRF) cruiser/racer. It's fun to sail and easy to handle, with accommodations for weekend cruising. J/33s have won major races on the East and West coasts of the United States and in the Great Lakes.

Coastal Cruising

Easy to handle, fast, and comfortable, the J/145 is built from a long-lasting, high-tech laminate using Toray unidirectional carbon fiber and E-glass skins, with Baltek Superlight 45 core, infused with TPI's patented SCRIMP system.

Closer to home, Ed and Cindy Huckins spend summers cruising the California coast from Redondo Beach to San Francisco Bay in the north and as far south as Ensenada, Mexico, in their 1987 J/40, *Mal de Mer III*. They've been exploring those Pacific waters for well over 15 years, and *Mal de Mer III* has racked up in excess of 15,000 miles in the process.

The width of a continent away, Steve Blecher and his crew of family and friends make similar annual voyages—in their case along the New England coast and beyond—in Steve's J/160, *Javelin*. Launched in August 1998, *Javelin* sailed out of Pilot's Point Marina in Westbrook, Connecticut, that summer on a cruise to Nantucket and Martha's Vineyard. A year later, Blecher and his crew sailed to Provincetown, on Cape Cod, and up to Maine, where they gunkholed along the coast between Penobscot Bay and Mount Desert Island. On the return voyage, *Javelin* called in at Harpswell Sound and Portsmouth, New Hampshire, plus Scraggy

Neck, Massachusetts. Steve Blecher said of his summer cruises, "On our trips to Maine, we do an overnight passage direct to the mid-coast of Maine, making our landfall between Harpswell Sound and Northeast Harbor."

In 2001, *Javelin*'s Maine cruise continued beyond Northeast Harbor on Mount Desert Island to the Canadian Maritimes, where *Javelin* braved the monumental tides (up to 40 feet) in the Bay of Fundy to reach Digby, Nova Scotia, and visit St. Andrews, New Brunswick, on the other side of the bay. Homebound, she called in at Campobello Island.

In addition to her annual Maine cruises, *Javelin* has sailed the New England coast out of Westbrook, Connecticut, to ports such as Mystic, Connecticut, and Narragansett Bay, Rhode Island, as well as Sag Harbor and Shelter Island off the east end of Long Island, and south to New York City. Steve Blecher said of his J/160: "All in all, she has been a great boat to sail and cruise. Most particularly because *Javelin* will sail in lighter and medium winds when most other boats are under power."

On the 2004 cruise to Maine, log-keeper Rick Van Mell echoed Blecher's statement when he noted as they passed Block Island, Rhode Island: "Now it was a pure beat upwind trying to make a course of 090 degrees with the wind from exactly that direction. *Javelin* was in her element in the ten- to thirteen-knot wind. Her bow sliced effortlessly through the small seas, with foam hissing along the lee side and occasional spray flying as she split the bigger waves."

Bob Johnstone is a firm believer in the delights of cruising the New England coast. He said: "There are so many coves and interesting places to explore in New England. It's a great cruising ground."

Bill Jacobsen and Renee Bushey took their J/46 *Vanish* on an 18-month circumnavigation of the Atlantic, including an extended cruise in the Mediterranean and the Caribbean. As with many other J boat owners, Bill and Renee entered races whenever they could. In March 2004, they finished third out of 18 boats in the Spinnaker 4 Class in the Heineken Regatta in St. Martin.

As this book went to press, the first J/65, a 64.5-foot cruiser, was gradually taking shape at the Pearson Composites factory in Warren and slated for a West Coast launch in the fall of 2005, with Rod Johnstone flying out to conduct the sea trials personally.

It is inevitable that more and more J cruiser owners will venture far offshore in the next few years. If there are any ports tucked away behind remote headlands that have never seen a J boat, they will soon.

J/Boats built the J/37c as a performance cruising version of the J/37 cruiser/racer. Jeff Johnstone said: "The biggest difference between the two boats is that the J/37c's cabin truck was extended 11 inches aft, which enlarged the aft cabin. Plus, the engine was moved from the middle of the boat to below the companionway steps, and the galley is bigger."

The J/42 can accommodate two couples, each with their own privacy, for a cruise, whether coastal or offshore. As a live-aboard, this 42-footer has plenty of space for a couple dedicated to the cruising lifestyle for months at a time.

This live-aboard cruiser, the J/130, is also a high-performance racer equipped with a carbon-fiber retractable J/Sprit and an asymmetrical spinnaker for downwind performance.

Opposite page: The J/37c variant of the J/37 was a concerted effort to maximize the cruising potential of an already successful boat.

Seven

Reaching New Heights

The first new design for the 1990s from the J/Boats design team was the J/35c (a cruising version of the highly successful J/35), which came out in June 1990. It was followed by the J/39 in September. Exactly one year later, the J/105 put in an appearance. The first of the "decimeter" yachts produced by J/Boats, it measured 34.5 feet LOA, or 10.5 meters—hence its designation as J/105. For many racers, it was love at first sight.

In his beautiful full-color book, *The World's Best Sailboats*, Volume II, noted yachtsman and boat builder Ferenc Máté commented of the J/Boats fleet, "Without doubt, the fastest and most fun-to-sail line of high-quality boats in the world."

Opposite page:
The 48-foot-LOA carbon-fiber J/145 is quick off the mooring for a big boat. Two people can go sailing in minutes. Simply hoist the main on a 2:1 halyard, cast off, and sail under main alone or unroll the jib. Flying the spinnaker is just as easy—it's contained in a snuffer sock and released from the cockpit.

That's high praise indeed from an astute and extremely knowledgeable yachtsman. After sailing on a J, Máté wrote of his experience: "In mid-afternoon, in 20-plus knots of wind, Jeff [Johnstone] and I took the [J] 105 sailing. He had the sails up and us underway before I could lash the dinghy to the buoy. The boat flew. I tried steering with my eyes closed and could not go off our sail setting—I sensed the resistance both ways in the helm. But J boats are not for everyone—you need strong neck muscles. Otherwise, in a gust, when the boat takes off like a bat out of hell, you're liable to get whiplash."

The J/105 introduced the carbon-fiber retractable bowsprit, and it features an asymmetrical spinnaker for ease of handling by two people. An article in *SAIL* magazine referred to the J/105 as "a two-person one-design sport cruiser that will keep up with a fully crewed IMS boat."

"When the J/105 appeared on the scene, it had very strong early acceptance. That hit a lull in the third year, then got a second wind and sales doubled," said Jeff Johnstone. Today, the J/105 is a recognized one-design class with large fleets on Chesapeake Bay, San Francisco Bay, and Long Island Sound. More than 630 J/105s sail in 17 countries.

The 30-foot J/92 arrived in time for 1992's sailing season in New England. This performance racer, equipped like the J/105 with a retractable bowsprit—now branded as a "J/Sprit"—and asymmetrical spinnaker, is user-friendly and, as expected, fun to sail.

At the end of the 1992 sailing season in Newport, the first J/130 was launched. Rod designed her primarily as a live-aboard cruiser, yet two people can handle this 43-footer comfortably at racing speeds. Rock singer Bob Seger owns a J/130, which he and his crew race regularly on the Great Lakes.

New Building Methods

Until 1994, most fiberglass boats were built following a standard practice. First, a female mold was built for the hull and a layer of gel coat sprayed in. Then, layers of fiberglass (mats) in resin were gradually built up to the required thickness. If the hull design called for

J/105 hull number 1
slices through the water.
Over 630 additional
J/105s have joined this
one since the design
was launched in
September 1991.
Sailing World magazine
chose the J/105 as
"Boat of the Year" in
its category for 1992.

a core material, such as balsa, outer skin layers of fiberglass and resin were laid in place, followed by the core material, then the inner skin, also of fiberglass and resin.

TPI Composites began employing the SCRIMP process for fiberglass construction on J boats in 1994. SCRIMP is an acronym for Seemann Composites Resin Infusion Molding Process. In simple terms, the process involves placing the entire laminate and core in the mold dry. Technicians place a vacuum bag over the lay-up and seal it to it. A pump then sucks all air from the bag, creating a vacuum. Technicians then introduce enough resin through a series of channels and spread throughout to wet the laminate, with the bag constantly under vacuum. Among the advantages for boating applications are: the vacuum

The first of the "decimeter" yachts from J/Boats, the J/105 has proven its racing ability in major one-design events like the North American Championship on San Francisco Bay in 2000.

Ever since its launching, the J/105 has shown its speed. One report claimed, "A gust of wind, blowing about 25 miles per hour, accelerated the J/105 up to a sustained speed of over 14 knots." The retractable carbon-fiber J/Sprit can be clearly seen here.

removes air and gases, thereby eliminating voids; the resin is driven uniformly throughout the part, providing a consistent laminate; and parts built by this process are lighter and stronger.

An additional eight J/Boat designs came on the market in the 1990s. Among them were a new and impressive line of ocean cruisers, the J/42, J/160, J/110, J/32, and J/46. A new L version (for "live aboard") of the J/42 joined them in 2000. The far-reaching voyages of some of them are featured in Chapter 6.

Carbon fiber is the latest medium for boat building. Everett Pearson first employed carbon fiber to manufacture tennis rackets in 1968 or 1969. "In the early days," he said, "carbon fiber cost $375 per pound." The price has come down considerably since then, but it is still an expensive material. Pearson first used the medium in boat building on the Etchells-Pearson 46, when he introduced a carbon-fiber backbone to the yacht.

Everett Pearson expressed his own reservations about the use of carbon fiber. "I was never a fan of carbon fiber for use in J boats," Pearson said. "To do an all carbon-fiber laminate is too cost prohibitive. The immediate result would be a considerable reduction in sales due." He explained that a boat built of carbon fiber, instead of the by-now traditional fiberglass, would be three or four times more expensive.

Despite Everett Pearson's concerns about the cost of the medium for boat building, carbon-fiber construction for J/Boats began in 1998 with the J/90. Prior to that, other boats in the line had already been built with some carbon-fiber content. Retractable bowsprits, made of carbon fiber, date back to 1991. Carbon-fiber masts started with the J/120 in 1994, and now most models are equipped with them. Carbon fiber is used extensively in the hull and deck laminates of the J/125 (1998), the J/145 (2000), and the J/65 (2005).

Carbon-fiber reinforced composites are often stronger than steel and considerably lighter, a definite advantage for a racing sailboat. While carbon fiber's light weight and inherent strength make it a considerable improvement over aluminum—the normal material for mast construction—it does have potential drawbacks. Aluminum will dent if struck hard but will stay intact, whereas carbon fiber is more likely to shatter. It is, however, becoming a popular construction material when weight and strength are important. Today, carbon fiber is used in aircraft and space shuttle parts, racing car construction—particularly Formula 1— motorcycles, bicycles, snowboards, and a plethora of other modern products, including golf clubs and tennis rackets.

J/Boats returned to its racing roots in 1997 with the application of SCRIMP and carbon technology to an experimental racing design: the J/90, a lightweight stripped-out 30-foot day racer with minimal accommodations and a large asymmetrical spinnaker flown from a sprit. Although the cost proved too high to sell more than a handful—due to the carbon hull, deck, rig, rudder, and nickel-aluminum-bronze keel strut—the J/90 paved the way for the two fastest J designs to date. The J/125, a 41-foot offshore sport boat, was launched in 1998, and the J/145, a 48-foot ocean cruiser/racer, was launched in 2000. Both these designs have proved their mettle in spectacular fashion on race courses around the globe.

After taking the new high-performance boat out for a test sail, John Kretschmer wrote, "The J/125 makes you feel young all over again." Surprisingly, the J/125 did not sell in large numbers, but it did win races. *Raincloud*, a J/125 from Texas, owned and skippered by Mike Rose, won the Chicago Mackinac Race in 1999, taking first place in its class and in the fleet.

The J/145 lived up to its early hype by finishing first and second in its class in the strenuous 2003 Fastnet Race, and first and

A 43-foot live-aboard cruiser with racing spirit, the J/130 is comfortable for two people to sail, even at racing speeds. The design features the retractable carbon-fiber J/Sprit and asymmetrical spinnaker for ease of handling and improved downwind performance.

second overall in the Cowes–Dinard–St. Malo classic across the English Channel. Royal Ocean Racing Club (RORC) Vice Commodore Chris Bull's J/145, *Jazz*, collected a hat trick of second-place-overall finishes, those being in the 704-mile Round Ireland Race, the 735-mile Cascais Race, and the 606-mile Middle Sea Race (in the Mediterranean). The latter race gave crews

of all boats a night to remember when a cold front passed over the fleet. With it came wind gusts up to 38 knots, accompanied by sheet lightning, fork lightning, thunder, and heavy rain. Trimmer Jerry Eplett, on *Jazz*, was reported to have complained, "I've never been blinded whilst sailing at night before." The RORC named the J/145 Overall IRC Boat of the Year.

The Wins Keep Coming

By the end of the 1990s, J/Boats had collected another shelf of awards from boating publications. *Sailing World* bestowed the honor of Overall Boat of the Year on the J/44 and the J/92. In addition, six other J boats picked up "Best of" awards from *Sailing World*. In the first five years of the 2000s, J/Boats continued to

shine by earning Best Overall for the J/133 and the J/100, plus two other "Best of" titles.

Meanwhile, production of J/105s reached hull number 400 and European construction got underway. For the first time, a new J boat, the J/109, was built in Europe before being built in the United States. Jeff Johnstone explained: "It was mainly because the European dealers and owners were first to identify the need for a boat in this size range that could win the top racing events, but also be comfy as well for a family cruise. In general in Europe, there is more dual-purpose use of boats; possibly due to the fact that more people rely on them as the weekend home."

The European dealers knew what they wanted and they got it. The J/109 was launched with anticipated sales success. A year later, the 109 plugs were shipped to Newport for TPI to commence American

A J/80 flies an asymmetrical spinnaker. The International J/80 Class Association is an ISAF-recognized class. The 2005 J/80 Worlds were due to be held in England, at Falmouth, on the rugged south coast of Cornwall.

A J/120 heading out for a race at Tortola in the British Virgin Islands. *Cruising World* magazine voted the J/120 "Overall Boat of the Year" and "Best Value" in a full-size cruising boat.

With spinnaker set, a J/120 speeds past Tortola, British Virgin Islands. Over 140 of these lithe 40-footers have been built. Ten out of 30 J/120 buyers in California are said to be first-time sailboat owners.

Close-up detail of a J/120 bow, showing its retractable J/Sprit with asymmetrical spinnaker and the roller-furling jib.

Launched in October 1994, the J/110 measures 36 feet LOA. As with other J/Sprit boats, there is no need for any crew member to go on deck to deploy the spinnaker—it is held in a snuffer sock and released from the cockpit.

Two J/80s set their spinnakers at the start of a downwind run in choppy race conditions during the AYC 2002 J/80 Circuit Regatta.

production. To date, 60 percent of the J/109s produced have been built in Europe, and the balance in the United States.

Between 2000 and the end of 2004, J boats of many sizes contended for a long list of yacht races in the world and won a large number of them. J boats also did well in the AZAB race from the United Kingdom to the Azores and back. More wins came in the Mediterranean. A J/109 won the Double-Handed Round Britain

Race overall and, across the English Channel, the French honored the design with the Copa Atlantique for the best performance in France by any design. Js won the Marblehead, Massachusetts, to Halifax, Nova Scotia; the Swiftsure in British Columbia; plus the Newport–Ensenada race.

The summer of 2003 celebrated the 25th anniversary of the J/24 Class at Newport. In Toronto at the same time, 27 J/35s marked

J/Boats' president, Jeff Johnstone, addresses invited guests and onlookers at the official launch of the J/160 in Newport, Rhode Island.

The retractable 6.25-foot-long J/Sprit can be seen to advantage as two J/80s fly their asymmetrical spinnakers at the beginning of the downwind leg of a race.

20 years of production by competing in the North American Championship on Lake Ontario. Also, in Rhode Island, a 43-foot J/133 stood waiting in its cradle to be introduced. Tooled in the United States, the cruiser/racer's plugs then went to France so J/Boats could build the new boat in both countries at the same time. In 2005, a French-built J/133 would win the prestigious Spi Ouest Regatta at La Trinité, France, over tough competition.

"The Sweetest Boat"

When the J/100 appeared in 2004, Bob Johnstone said, "It's the best-looking J boat yet."

"Every boat we design and produce is one that someone in the company wants for their own," said Jeff Johnstone. His cousin Drake agreed. Speaking of the J/100 and his father's involvement in the design, Drake said: "His [Bob's] energy in putting forward new concepts, such as the 100, is strong. He believed in the [J/100] concept highly."

Bob displayed his faith in the J/100 by taking delivery of hull number 1. "Because that was the boat he wanted to own," Jeff said.

The J/Boats team designed this handsome 33-footer for the day and weekend sailing markets, and for the single hander. She's long and narrow and designed for speed on all points of sail. For rainy days and cold winds, a full-width dodger gives protection from the weather. Relatively Spartan below decks, the J/100 does

Sailing World magazine gave the J/160 an affectionate nod by naming it "Boat of the Year" for 1997. Solidly built, rugged in character, yet elegant under sail, the J/160 is a true world cruiser.

From any angle, the 53-foot J/160 is an impressive cruising boat. It was designed primarily for comfortable, fast, ocean-going cruises for a short-handed crew, yet can accommodate six in three cabins.

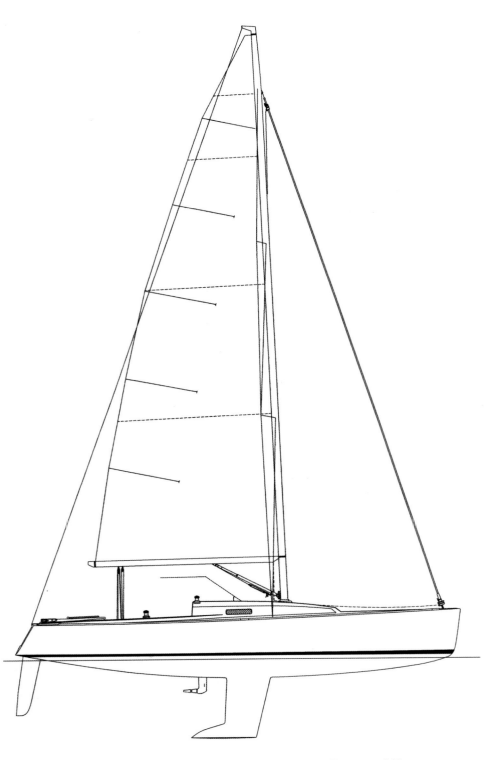
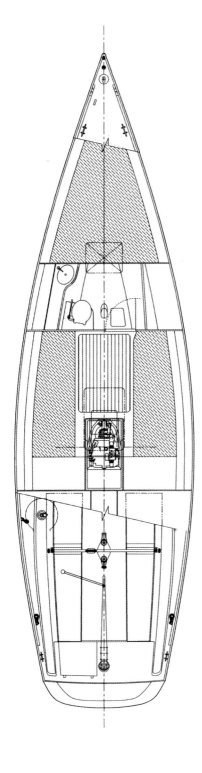

J/100 Principal Dimensions

LOA	32.8 feet	10.00 meters	I	38.5 feet	11.73 meters
LWL	29.0 feet	8.84 meters	ISP	43.0 feet	31.11 meters
Beam	9.3 feet	2.82 meters	J	11.5 feet	3.51 meters
Standard draft	5.8 feet	1.75 meters	P	38.0 feet	11.58 meters
Standard ballast	2,500 pounds	1,134 kilograms	E	13.5 feet	4.11 meters
Displacement	6,500 pounds	2,948 kilograms	SA/Dspl	22	22
Engine	10 horsepower	10 horsepower	Dspl/L	119	119
100% SA	478 square feet	44.40 square meters			

The elegant curve of a carbon-fiber mast on Steve Blecher's J/160, *Javelin*.

A roomy performance cruiser, the J/32 is Alan Johnstone's first solo design. Alan said his criteria were, "that the boat should sail well and handle well. It was targeted to younger families with children as an entry-level boat, and for older sailors who may have tired of bigger boats and want to step down in size."

have two berths and a marine head, with a forward V-berth as an option. A 10-horsepower auxiliary diesel with folding propeller is standard equipment. The first J/100 hull took to the water in June 2004. Rod and Bob took her out on sea trials from her launching point in Barrington, Rhode Island, and sailed her down Narragansett Bay to Newport. At the end of an exhilarating run, they pronounced themselves extremely satisfied with their new release. *Sailing World* magazine liked it too; they voted the new J/100 Overall Boat of the Year for 2005.

John Johnstone had his own compliment for the J/100. After talking about the beauty and style of Herreshoff designs, he said, "[sailing] the J/100 is like sailing a Herreshoff."

Although J/Boats brings out new models on a regular basis, the models tend to stay in production longer than their competitors.

The J/90 is a lightweight, stripped-out, 30-foot day racer with minimal accommodation. *Sailing World* magazine voted this high-performance yacht "Sport Boat of the Year" for 1998.

Alan Johnstone's second design for J/Boats was the J/109, designed and built for the European market initially to fill a specific need. It is now built in France and in the United States.

"The average life of a [J] design is six point five to seven years; certainly in excess of six years," Jeff Johnstone said. "The industry standard is three to four years."

Early in 2005, Tom Babbitt, long-time J boat fan and owner of a J/42, said of the new J/100: "The J/100 is the sweetest boat I have ever sailed. If I could afford to have a J/42 and a 100, I would."

Like the various members of the Johnstone family, many of whom have owned large numbers of J boats since the first production J/24 came off the line, Tom and Jane Babbitt have owned nine Js. In order they are J/30, J/35, J/37, J/40, J/34c, J/22, J/35, J/34c, and J/42. "Effectively,"

Tom said, "we have owned three J models twice each. In all we've owned over 300 feet of J boats." (The actual figure is just over 312 feet.)

From One Success to the Next

Two hundred ninety boats from 34 states and 14 countries entered the popular 2005 Key West Race Week. J boats accounted for almost one-third of the total, including 40 entries in the J/105 class. As one would expect, the Js acquitted themselves well. Jim Johnstone, J/Boats' sales manager, took third place in the J/105 One-Design series with his USA332. Out of 10 boats entered in Division 2, in the

Continued on page 153

The high-tech J/90 features a carbon-fiber hull, deck, rig, and rudder. Fitted with a retractable J/Sprit and asymmetrical spinnaker, this 27-foot-LWL racer weighs in at only 3,100 pounds.

At 41 feet LOA, the J/125 is a prize-winning sport boat. *Sailing World* magazine voted it "PHRF/Sport Boat of the Year" for 1999. A feature article on the award noted that "the long, lean, and mean J/125 simply blew away its competition."

A J/109 under construction at Pearson Composites in Warren, Rhode Island. The hull is built using the SCRIMP molding process. All joinery work takes place at the factory.

A racer, pure and high-tech: J/125s have won the Chicago–Mackinac Race, and Class A PHRF of the Ft. Lauderdale–Key West Race, among others. With a capacious cockpit stretching more than a third of the boat's length, there's plenty of room for a full racing crew.

The deck mold of a J/109—the deck is laminated in the mold in the inverted position using the SCRIMP process. When set, the mold is removed and the deck turned right-side up.

A J/133 at speed with asymmetrical spinnaker set. Tooled in the United States, the J/133's plugs were sent to France so J/Boats could build the cruiser/racer in both countries at the same time.

A J/133 under construction at Pearson Composites in Warren, Rhode Island. The hull has been completed and all interior joinery work is being installed. First launched in September 2003, the 43-foot-LOA J/133 is a cruiser/racer with offshore cruising capability.

PHRF-2 class, the J/133s took second, fifth, and eighth, plus a J/44 took seventh place. That second-place finish went to Mike Rose of Houston, Texas, with *Raincloud*, namesake of the J/125 that won the Chicago–Mackinac Race for Rose in 1999.

Sixteen J/80s challenged each other in their one-design event, with Rick Schaffer's *C'est Nasty* becoming the eventual winner. And eight J/29s fought for honors in their one-design series, which was won easily by John and Tony Esposito in *Hustler*. George Petrides of New York City won the J/120 class in *Avra*, and Bill Sweetser's *Rush* took the J/109 win home to Annapolis, Maryland.

As 2005 dawned, two large hulls took shape at the factory in Warren. Dubbed the "ultimate private sailing yacht" by J/Boats, Inc., the two semi-custom-built J/65s were due for completion a few months later, in time to sail away in the fall. At 64.5 feet on deck and 57 feet on the water line, the J/65 has a beam of 16 feet and a 9-foot draft keel. After she's rolled out of the factory, J/65 hull number 1 will be shipped to the West Coast

for sea trials, where Rod Johnstone will be at the helm and other J/Boats executives on hand. Following the sea trials, she will be handed over to her owner, who plans to cruise from California to Hawaii for the boat's maiden ocean voyage. Hull number 2, by comparison, has a 12-foot draft racing keel. She has been purpose-built to take part in offshore races on the East Coast, the Caribbean, and California waters.

The success of the J/100 in 2004 augurs well for the next decimeter design. The J/124, scheduled to make its first appearance at East Coast boat shows in the fall of 2005, is a handsome 40-footer. It's a larger version of the J/100 with a few refinements, including a wheel to replace the tiller, a small galley and chart table, enclosed head and shower, plus 6 feet standing head room.

Even with the regular introduction of new and better designs, J boat aficionados still enjoy the original J/24. Eric Cressy, publisher of *SAIL* magazine, sent Jeff Johnstone the following message in March 2005: "Jeff, I thought you'd get a kick out of this. Just purchased my

When completed, the J/133's cabin is well proportioned and carefully appointed for cruising.

The J/100 has a large cockpit for day and weekend sailing. Single-handed sailing is easy and fun as the boat proves to be quick in light winds and stable in a breeze.

eighth J/24 this week as a 40th B-Day present to myself. [I] Paid a whole $1,000 for a nice spring project to keep me out of the bars. I plan to teach my kids how to sail on it like my sailmaker dad taught me."

"Our philosophy is based on the 'Gee, wouldn't it be nice to have a boat like this' comments," said Bob. "With the years of sailing experience we have, if Rod likes it and I get enthusiastic about it, and the other guys like it,

it's probably going to be a good boat, because our standards of reference for what we've been creating are fairly high. So if we find something we like better than what we already have, there's a high probability of success."

As J/Boats, Inc. goes from one success to the next, the future of the company looks bright. Perhaps Bob Johnstone summed it up best when he said, "It's all about keeping the joy in sailing."

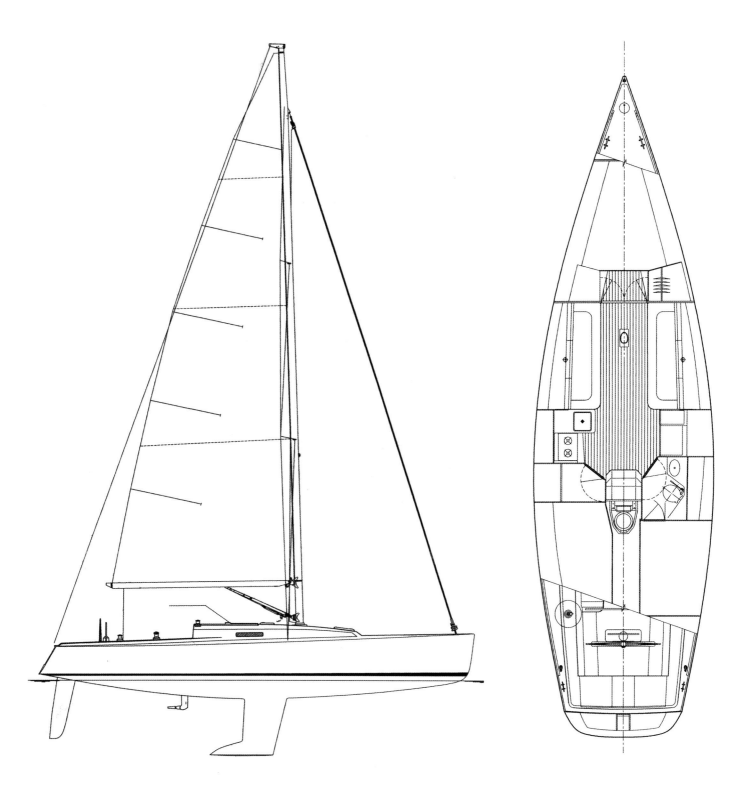

J/124 Principal Dimensions

LOA	40.70 feet	12.40 meters	100% SA	754 square feet	70.04 square meters
LWL	36.20 feet	11.03 meters	I	49.00 feet	14.94 meters
Beam	11.33 feet	3.45 meters	ISP	54.70 feet	16.67 meters
Standard draft	6.90 feet	2.10 meters	J	14.00 feet	4.27 meters
Standard ballast	5,000 pounds	2,268 kilograms	P	48.40 feet	14.75 meters
Displacement	11,500 pounds	5,216 kilograms	E	17.00 feet	5.18 meters
Engine	40 horsepower	40 horsepower	SA/Dspl	24	24
			Dspl/L	108	108

When the J/100 sailed for the first time, Bob Johnstone said, "It's the best-looking J boat yet." He took hull number 1 of the handsome 33-footer for his own use. *Sailing World* magazine voted the J/100 "Overall Boat of the Year" for 2005.

The ultimate private sailing yacht, the J/65 cruising/racing sloop is 64.5 feet LOA. Destined for a West Coast launch and sea trials, the first J/65 was scheduled for a Pacific crossing from California to Hawaii soon after.

Another new design, the J/124 is a 40-foot "weekending" day sailer. A longer version of the J/100 with a large destroyer wheel instead of a tiller, it also has a small galley, a chart table, enclosed head and shower, and 6 feet standing head room.

Appendix
Chronological History of J/Boats Designs

Designation	LOA (in feet)	Year	Launch Month
International J/24	24	1977	March
J/23x (daggerboard)	23	1977	July
J30 prototype	29.9	1978	May
J/30	29.9	1979	January
J/36	36	1980	July
J/29	29.5	1982	June
International J/22	22.5	1983	May
J/35	35.4	1983	June
J/41 IOR	41	1983	December
J/27	27.5	1984	June
J/34 IOR	34	1985	March
J/40	40.3	1985	April
J/28	28.5	1986	June
J/37	37.5	1986	October
J/34c	34.2	1987	June
J/33	33.5	1988	June
J/44	44.9	1989	May
J/37c	37.5	1989	May
J/35c	35.2	1990	June
J/39	39.5	1990	September
J/105	34.5	1991	September
J/92	30	1992	June
J/130	42.8	1992	October
International J/80	26.2	1993	April
J/120	40	1994	January
J/110	36	1994	October
J/42	42	1995	June
J/160	52.8	1995	December
J/32	32.5	1996	August
J/90	30	1997	August
J/125	41	1998	June
J/46	46	1999	June
J/145	48	2000	May
J/109	35.5	2001	August
J/133	43	2003	September
J/100	32.8	2004	July
J/65	64.9	2005	August
J/124	40.7	2005	September

Photo Credits

MBI Publishing Company would like to thank the following for providing photographs and/or drawings:

Cabot, Edmund: pages 123, 124
Crowhurst, Steve: author photo, front flap
Dalton, Anthony: pages 8 (top), 45 (top), 48, 49 (bottom), 50, 54, 90, 103 (bottom), 104, 105, 111 (top), 112–116, 118, 119, 122 (bottom), 150 (bottom), 151 (bottom), 152 (bottom)
Grenon, Fran, Spectrum Photo: front cover and page 3
J/Boats, Inc.: pages 1, 5–8 (bottom), 9, 10, 12–22, 24 (top center, bottom), 25–34, 36–44, 46, 47, 49 (top), 51–53, 55, 56, 58–61, 63, 65–82, 84, 85, 86–90, 91–100, 102, 103 (top), 106–110, 111 (bottom), 117, 120, 121, 122 (top), 125, 126, 128–130, 132–137, 139–141, 143 (top), 144, 145, 146 (bottom), 147, 148 (top), 149, 150 (top), 151 (top), 152 (top), 153–157, 159
Johnstone, Lucia: page 24 (top left)
Jonas, Hank: page 146 (top)
McDonald, Bruce: pages 138, 142, 143 (bottom)
Pearson Composites: page 24 (top right)
Read, Ken: page 48 (bottom)
Walker, Mike: pages 62, 64
Warburton, Mike: page 148 (bottom)

A J/90 at speed flying a pale green spinnaker on a downwind run.

Index